CLARK & REINFRANK
Wisdom Wit & Wine

KARIN CLARK & ARNO REINFRANK

WISDOM WIT AND WINE

- My Funny Palatine -

A Dictionary of South West German Vernacular and Fun

Hermann G. Klein Verlag
1994

Die Erstauflage dieses Buches erschien 1982
by Oswald Wolff (Publishers) Ltd., London
ISBN 0-85496-366-9

Titelbild: Armin Hott

1994
3. Auflage

Neufferstraße 2, 67346 Speyer
Druck: Robert Weber, Offsetdruck, 67346 Speyer
Buchbinderei: Osswald & Co., 67433 Neustadt/Wstr.
ISBN 3-921797-41-1

This booklet was written because nothing like it has been written before.

It deals with words of a peculiar German dialect used by a population of unusual characteristics. It deals with a landscape bordering in the east on the Rhine and in the west on France. The inhabitants of that region produce sweet wine, smelly chemicals and any other goods one may think of. The present system of administration grew out of the councils created by Napoleon. Family names are reminders of the keen interest in the riches of this area taken by various Bavarian kings, who sent their officials to collect taxes. The deep woods of the central mountain range, the *Pfälzerwald,* hide American defence installations today. Sometimes the army unearths foundations of barracks which once housed Roman legions. There are remnants of more than three hundred castles and fortifications. Two world-famous cathedrals in the old cities of *Speyer* and *Worms* compete with the gigantic plants of the BASF *Ludwigshafen* for public attention of a differing kind. The former call for admiration, the latter must be sniffed.

In short, this booklet deals with the *Pfalz* in the south-west of Germany.

Pfalz rhymes with 'cults' or 'shmultz'. In contrast to Yiddish, from which the English language borrows *shmaltz* as well as the adjective *shmaltzy,* the adjective to *Pfalz* is *Pfälzisch* (to rhyme with shall-fish), and not *Pfalzy.*

The men and women who are Pfälzisch, talk Pfälzisch, laugh Pfälzisch, are known as the Palatinates or the *Pfälzer. Pfalz*, the word itself, has the same root as the English 'palace', and originally meant an *imperial* or *royal castle* serving as court of justice. Later it designated a *county palatine*, and today it is the *Palatinate* part of the Federal German state of *Rhineland-Palatinate*.

The *Pfälzer* display many linguistic peculiarities useful to know for any visitor from foreign shores. Yet there is a lot more to be said about them for reasons best explained in the following story.

Mrs. Schneider was invited to a coffee party in Wiesbaden. Soon she had arrested everyone's attention with exciting accounts of the *Pfälzer*. They, she vivaciously maintained, were so kind to each other, so industrious and helpful, witty and communicative, simply lovable.

Her listeners gasped. Never before had they realized what charming compatriots were living to the south. A mere hour away by rail or car! And to crown it all, Mrs. Schneider insisted that the most warm-hearted and charitable of *Pfälzer* were to be found in the industrial city of *Ludwigshafen*.

Finally, when she had to catch her breath, one lady in the party timidly asked:

'Well, and you, where do you come from?' Mrs. Schneider – blushing with modesty – had to admit: 'I . . . come from Ludwigshafen . . . '

Abbedid

pronounced 'ubba-did' to rhyme with 'rub a lid'. High German: Appetit. English: Appetite.

Abbedid is not just a craving for food, or a common reaction of the taste buds to an appetizing smell from the kitchen. To the Pfälzer it is a sensation of delight they expect you to display any time they make you face a full plate. If instead you turn green, you will give cause for the greatest concern regarding the state of your health. To suffer from loss of *Abbedid* is unforgivable. Showing a good *Abbedid* will reassure everybody that you are in epicurean harmony with the world. Come what may after you've satisfied their expectation, as long as your *Abbedid* is alright, there is hope for you and your future.

Around the Pfälzische dinner table nobody (of good German manners) starts eating before everyone else is ready to begin. The word for 'go' is *Guude Abbedid*! (pronounced 'ghouda ubba-did'), a kind of well-wishing that amounts to an agnostic way of saying pre-dinner grace. Where grace is said, *Guude Abbedid*! follows, regardless of the fact that both formulae only tend to delay the tucking in.

The response expected is *Dankschee, gleichfalls* (pronounced 'dunk-sha(y), gly*ch*-ful(t)s' with the *ch* sounding like in the Scottish word 'ni*ch*t' –Thank you, the same to you).

Should you happen to order a meal in a Pfälzische

restaurant, the waitress' friendly wish of *Guude Abbe did* may be echoed far and near, or may be slightly changed into an abbreviated *Än Guude*! (pronounced 'ai(r)n ghouda'). It means the same and accordingly calls for the same response: *Dankschee, gleichfalls*.

If your thanks to the well-wishers is very friendly, you may be drawn into one of the very Pfälzische conversations which result in everything on your plate getting cold. You'd better leave out the *gleichfalls* (the same to you), if the others are merely sitting in front of their glasses. Otherwise they may conclude that you are a foreigner.

Mrs. Zimmermann was worried about her son's shyness, when it came to meeting the other sex. She decided to pull a bit of her own weight on his behalf. Then a young lady from the neighbouring village finally agreed to see her son and Mrs. Zimmermann accompanied him to her house.

'But Mum,' her son said, 'what am I to say to the girl . . . ?' Impatienty Mrs. Zimmermann cried out: 'Tell her "When I look into your eyes, I neither want to eat nor drink anymore" . . .'

Left alone with the girl in the back garden, young Mr. Zimmermann pulled himself together.

'Miss,' he uttered, clearing his throat of all inhibitions, 'when I look at you, I lose all my *Abbedid* . . .'

Abbedid can get larger than life at times. *Paul Münch*, the late Pfälzer ballad writer, most poetically described the intrusion of a fierce dragon into the peace of a village in the Pfalz:

> Acht Zentner Werscht sin do verschwunn
> in Zeit vun eener Vertelschtunn
>
> Eight hundredweight of sausage to devour
> took him one quarter of an hour.

This called for Siegfried of Nibelungen fame to enter and once and for all kill the fierce dragon. A jubilant population thanked him by inaugurating a week-long festival to celebrate his victory. (See under letter D – *Derkemer Worschtmarkt.*) Quite a typical reaction for the Pfälzer who love to celebrate in style, and their style, as *Paul Münch* has shown, is quite baroque.

Alla, allee, alloo

pronounced 'ul-lah', 'ul-leh', 'ul-loh' to rhyme with 'colour', 'ballet', 'chapeau'. None of the words exists in High German. They are borrowed from the French 'aller' – to go.

Alla is without doubt the most favoured exclamation of any native Pfälzer. 'This,' a writer remarked long before the great influx of Turkish labourers in these parts, 'this makes the Pfalz the true country of Allah!'

All three varieties, *alle, allee* and *alloo*, are in constant use throughout the *Kurpfalz*, the former Electorate Palatine, which comprises the Palatinate on the left bank of the Rhine and roughly Mannheim and Heidelberg on the other side.

The adoption of these exclamations actually dates back to well before 1700, when the Kurpfalz was taken over by the French. As a whole series of encounters with the French forces of occupation ensued, the use of the words was re-enforced over and over again. (See also under L – *Lui*.) Or should we say that the persistent usage tells a lot about Pfälzer conservativism?

True to the French meaning of 'aller', *alla, alla hopp* or *allee hopp* call for immediate action: 'Let's go! Come on! Forward!' *Alla* in particular can acquire other connotations though, depending on the context and on the inflection. It may take the place of 'well then' in English.

'*Alla, adschee*!' (pronounced 'ul-lah, ud-sheh' – from

the French 'adieu' – good-bye) announces the intent of speedy departure. Faced with this threat a host will react at once by pleading: '*Alla*, bleibt noch ä bissel.' (pronounced 'ul-lah, blybt no*ch* /as in Scottish 'lo*ch*'/ ais bizzle' – come on, do stay a little longer).

On its own *alla* stands for a self-assertive rhetorical question: 'Didn't I say so?!' or 'Didn't I guess?!'

Alloo, mostly used to allay, will be employed to appease the guests who might show signs of imminent departure. '*Alloo*!' the host will utter and suggestively pull the cork from yet another bottle. And, be prepared, he may go in for several repetitions of this manoeuvre before the night is over. *Alla*!

Bidselwasser

pronounced 'bidsle-vusser' to rhyme with 'bristle cusser'. High German: Sprudelwasser. English: Soda water.

Anything that prickles, tickles, sparkles or bubbles the Pfälzer will call *Bidsel*. What better and more suggestive term could therefore be used to illustrate the effervescence of carbonated water than *Bidselwasser*?

A healthy Pfälzer will only resort to *Bidselwasser*, however, if he absolutely must, in case of a severe hangover or when driving, for instance. With the advent of the motor car as major means of transport, *Bidselwasser* became big business, too, and expensive. Some places will sell it at half the price they charge for a quarter liter of wine to make up for the loss in income from the Pfälzer's most favourite beverage.

There does exist yet another name for soda water, of interest from a historical point of view. When soda water bottles were still hand-made, the glass blowers managed to insert glass marbles into the bottles. The marble would, by force of the gaseous pressure, act as a stopper for as long as the bottle stood upright. When the bottle was toppled, the beverage could be poured freely. In honour of this ingenious invention carbonated water was known in the Pfalz as *Gliggerwasser* (pronounced 'gligger vusser', for the glass marble called *Gligger* in the vernacular).

You can still order *Gliggerwasser* and be served

sparkling soda water, even though you will look in vain for the *Gligger*. They have been replaced by other stopping devices. And with the introduction of machine-made bottles the glass blowers, too, have disappeared, these craftsmen who in masterly fashion were able to blow liter bottles, give or take no more than a two percent margin of error.

Before the 'no return' bottles came into use, on a hot summer day in the Pfalz, a friend of ours bought a bottle of ice-cold *Bidselwasser* at a kiosk. Taking no time to ask for a glass he started to drink straight from the bottle. His immediate reaction was one of disgust. The mouth of the bottle tasted and smelled terribly of nicotine. He then assumed – and was probably right – that a cigar smoker must have drunk from the bottle before him. The bottle had been returned properly and later re-filled improperly, without a good cleaning. Enraged our friend decided to write a letter of complaint to the bottling company and looked for the name and address on the label.

He got no further than the name of the company owner, and gave up. The man's name was – Max Swet.

May-be the Romans, who settled along the Rhine and discovered the original *Bidselwasser*, were right after all. They diverted the mineral springs to supply them with plenty of healthy water . . . in their bath houses.

Bierbrauer

pronounced 'beer brow-er' to rhyme with 'gear power'. High German: Bierbrauer. English: Brewer.

Reading over more than a thousand sagas and tales about people, places and events in the Pfalz, we did not come across one single mention of *Bier*. Plenty of references to wine and milk and water, but none to *Bier*.

This is all the more astonishing as the craft of brewing was introduced right along with Christianization by Irish and Scottish monks, probably as early as the turn of the 6th century, when Saint Leobardus founded the first monastery in these parts.

For centuries the brewing of beer remained a prerogative of the religious orders. By the 16th century, however, secular breweries had come into the picture. In *Frankenthal* a document dated 1550 specifically records the brewing rights of a private local establishment. This old Frankenthal brewery changed hands not long ago, when it was bought, in 1972, by the Federal Post Office. Should Pfälzer postmen – the world is left wondering – should they be the thirstiest of all civil servants to warrant such a take-over?

There are still a few old-style beer gardens around, decorated with garlands of multi-coloured lights and, naturally, a podium reserved for the brass band. But teams of heavy horses pulling loads and loads of barrels, once the trade mark of every brewery, have all but disappeared. Only the big companies nowadays can afford the luxury of displaying them on special occasions, during festivals or attractions of like power of advertising.

Bierbrauer and their deliverymen were known to be an extremely refined lot. As subtle as their manners were the references to their drinking capacity. You would get a pretty good idea about the latter – so the rule of thumb had it – if you gauged the amount of water their teams cascaded on to the road.

And whatever a Pfälzer *Bierbrauer* could manage, any other Pfälzer prided himself of drinking.

> Dorschtig wie ähn Mälzer –
> siehscht – des is ähn Pfälzer.
>
> (Thirsty as a malster is a real Pfälzer.)

Thus confirmed the poetic outpouring of a creative genius, whose name escaped mention.

Pfälzer beer drinkers have a peculiar way of reworking monetary value into their favourite currency.

'Just imagine, you would win 50.000 DM at the races!' one chap marvelled. 'So what.' the other put him down straight away. 'That's not much. It buys me 50.000 bottles of beer and doesn't leave a penny for food.'

Bollidsei

pronounced 'bolly-dzeye' to rhyme with 'jolly guy'. High German: Polizei. English: The police, the law.

Pfälzische grannies trying to control unruly young children may refer to the *Bollidsei* in a disciplinary threat. 'Dich holt de Schutzmann!' (Pronounced 'di*ch** hohlt da shoultsmunn' – The guardian of the law will arrest you, if you don't behave yourself.)

Later, should the teenager compete with his ancestors in the consumption of alcohol, the threat becomes more real. However, in a reported court case, where the charge was drunken driving, the judge, a Pfälzer by origin and nature, showed unusual insight into the constitution of his countryman. He ruled that the driver actually ought to be lauded for the amount of alcohol in his blood. Thanks only to his normal measure of intoxication had he been able to react quickly, avoid a bulldozer cutting into the main road from a country lane and save human life by wrapping his car around the next tree.

Nevertheless, care is recommended. Even Pfälzische judges can be unreliable in such circumstances. Gone are the days, when two *Bollidsischde* (pronounced 'bolly-dzischda' – policemen) politely helped a drunken man out of the pub and into his car, checked the

* 'di*ch*' as in the Scottish 'ni*ch*t'.

ignition for him, finally gave the car a downhill push for a start. If this tale does anything, it shows what the Pfälzer expect of their *Bollidsei.*

What they, or the *Bollidsei*, actually do get is another matter.

The *Bollidsei* is called to break up a brawl. In front of the notorious drinking place one *Bollidsischt* boasts to his fellow officers: 'I'll show you, how I deal with them single-handedly. You just keep count as they come catapulting out the door!' In he goes. Out comes number one. 'One!' the officers outside duly register – right into an all too familiar voice crying: 'Cut it out . . . It's me . . .'

With the development of industry and a proletariat confined to over-crowded quarters, pubs like the one mentioned were shooting up in the cities of Mannheim and Ludwigshafen. Meanwhile the *Bollidsei*, at least until 1918, were armed with sabres rather than with truncheons and pistols, and with a good sense of humour.

Well after midnight, a *Bollidsischt* on his beat encountered a Pfälzer holding fast to a house wall. 'My!' the *Bollidsischt* exclaimed, 'You have your tank full, haven't you?' The one so addressed looked the *Bollidsischt* up and down. Breathing heavily he responded: 'You see, I'm drunk, and that will be over by tomorrow. But you, you're with the *Bollidsei*, and that sticks forever . . .'

All in all, the Pfälzische *Bollidsei* is still remindful of the slogan – a wee bit waned now – under which they sailed during the past sixties and seventies: 'The police, your friend and helper!' Complaints against them by members of the public are considerably fewer in number than elsewhere.

Bredsel

pronounced 'bread-zell' to rhyme with 'red shell'. High German: Brezel or Prezel. From the Latin 'brachium' – arm. English: Pretzel or cracknel.

Fresh from the oven and still hot a Pfälzer *Bredsel* cracks and crackles under your bite. Plenty of salt crystals on its brown crust truly make the *Bredsel* a mouth-watering affair.

Shaped like the two intertwined arms of a pixy the *Bredsel* – to no-one's surprise – has a long history. It was found depicted on Egyptian pyramids even, and still plays a mysterious rôle in ancient rites. During 'Summer Day' processions, for instance, children (the only ones allowed by the Church to indulge in traditional heathen customs) will carry a *Bredsel* prepared as a sweet pastry and mounted on a stick wrapped in colourful paper garlands.

May it tally with history or not, folklore has preserved a different story of its origin. A baker journeyman gaoled for some misdemeanour had pleaded to the local overlord for mercy. But pardon would only be granted, he heard, if he could produce an absolutely new kind of bakery treat. How could he, in a world full of any imaginable type of bread, cake and pastry? Brooding in his cell, looking out through the bars of his window into vineyard after vineyard (which automatically localizes him in the Pfalz) he suddenly discovered a vine close by that had interlocked two of its creepers into the shape of . . . a *Bredsel*. That was it!

The football crowds of today, in the *Südwest-Stadion* of Ludwigshafen or elsewhere, have little use for stories like this. They yell their orders for *Bredseln* down to the vendors who carry loads of the pastry in wicker baskets. These vendors display remarkable skills in whirling the *Bredseln* overhead to the upper ranks like flying saucers, and likewise in catching the coins thrown down to them.

In Ludwigshafen and Mannheim *Bredseln* are sold in bakeries, in super-markets, in pubs and restaurants, on street corners. Unthinkable that you would have to look far for a *Bredsel* vendor, when you step out of the railway station in either town.

'Three for twenty!' (Pfennig) they used to cry in pre-inflation days. 'Drunk as a *Bredsel* vendor' recalls the days, when 'irregulars' carried their wares from pub to pub ending up in the last one with a terrible thirst. *Bredsel-merb* (pronounced 'bread-zell merrb' – as brittle as a *Bredsel*) describes the feeling of hunger pangs that come along with a good quenching of thirst.

'Irregulars' were also responsible for price-wars fought noisily not too long ago. Special underweight *Bredseln* were offered to the public at bargain prices, only to be under-cut by a challenging 'Seven for twenty!' Regardless of the financial loss driving off competition was a matter of honour as well as a question of survival.

It has been reported that during those times a vendor bought his *Bredseln* for three Pfennig a piece and sold them for two in fierce competition. 'How do you manage to stay in business?' he was asked. 'It's the turnover that will bring in the profit.' was his reply.

Speyer by the way, stages an annual *Bredsel Fest*.

Charles, Carl

first names of two historical personalities important to the Pfalz. High German: Karl. English: Charles. In Palatinate dialect the name will appear as Ka'l (pronounced 'cull'), *Galle* (pronounced 'gull-a') and *Gillegalle* (pronounced 'gill-agull-a').

While *Charles* and *Carl* would seem today to be high-brow versions of the more ordinary *Karl*, centuries ago these names gave account of the close political and cultural ties between what are now France and Germany, and reflect their joint root, the Latin name *Carolus*.

The most important one of the High Cs in terms of world history is without question *Charlemagne*, head of the Holy Roman Empire since 800, who started out as King of the Franks and after various conquests became the master of the Carolingian empire. *Carl Theodor*, Elector Palatine from 1742-1799, may lay claim to comparable significance, however, for the Pfalz proper.

Charlemagne, whose reign lasted from 742 till his death in 814, is rightfully called the creator of the Pfalz. Travelling widely throughout the sphere of his influence with his imperial entourage he established several administrative, judicial and cultural centres in strategic places, including one of these royal palaces (Palatium) in the territory of the present Pfalz. May it be noted that *Charlemagne's* chief adviser was the Yorkshireman and scholar Alcuin, considered the most renowned intellect of the time. And may it further be noted that the language spoken at *Charlemagne's* court, wherever it convened, was the Germanic dialect most clearly preserved in the Palatinate vernacular. Documents written during Carolingian rule – the 'Covenant of Strassburg of 842' as one example – will give evidence to this effect.

Though German history books now give his name as *Karl der Grosse*, you will know him as *Charles the Great, Charlemagne* or *Carolus Magnus*, with the C obviously dominating.

In the case of *Carl Theodor* the modernized spelling of *Karl* contradicts all traditional documents as well. His initials C.T. appear on every piece of china produced after 1762 in the Frankenthal porcelain manufacture. The manufacture had been in private hands before the elector bought it, and though it existed for no more than 44 years altogether, it gained world-wide reputation and its products are still in highest demand among collectors the world over.

Any *Charles* or *Carl* in the Pfalz today will answer to *Ka'l* or *Galle* or to the friendly teasing of *Gillegalle*. –The least favoured letter in the Palatinate alphabet, the letter 'r' being omitted in all three versions of the name *Karl*.

One of the most famous *Ka'ls* in the region must surely be 'de klää *Ka'l* von Mannem' (pronounced 'da cla(y) cull fon Munnem' – little Charles of Mannheim). The adjective before the name ironically underlines the weightiness of the so-called *Ka'l* (whose actual first name isn't *Ka'l* at all), a humorist of merit. 'My weight is 120 kg plus' (about 19 stones), he is reported to have said. 'But God help me, if I get angry, then I weigh twice as much.'

The blues singer Joy Fleming, born under a far less

flamboyant name in Mannheim and possessing a real Kurpfälzische intonation, immortalized a certain *Ka'l*, her fictional boyfriend, by describing his life style. He has left her a number of times and she even knows the address of 'the other woman' from the postman. But she loves him and consoles herself:

> If he's hungry or ill,
> he'll come back, sure he will . . .

Her record of this song became an immediate hit in the Pfalz and on the Kurpfälzisch-right bank of the Rhine. Miss Fleming studied the art of blues singing in American GI bars and is on record saying: 'If you work in such a place, you better not be just a wee little sausage.' By her looks and by the fortissimo of her voice, she isn't.

Karl Fink and Peter Schäfer of Mannheim (the latter known as 'Blume-Peter', as he would sell his flowers on street corners and in pubs) were once discussing the family background of the Elector Palatine *Carl Theodor*, the count to whom Mannheim owes so much. 'Do you know, what his family name was?' Peter enquired. 'Don't know,' *Ka'l* shrugged. 'He had none.' 'Know why?' Peter quipped. 'Prob'ly was illegitimate. Must have been happening in these circles, too!'

Derkem

pronounced 'dare-k-ham' to rhyme with 'spare-'hem'. High German: Bad Dürkheim, a Palatinate spa and wine-growing community.

During a period in time, when even the smallest villages in the Pfalz stage their own 'Wine Fest', the *Derkemer Worschtmarkt* (pronounced 'dare-k-ham'a vorscht mark(e)t' – Bad Dürkheim Sausage Fair) has been able to hold on to its age-old reputation and can still claim to be the greatest among all the other events.

This autumn festival of fun and food and wine takes place in and about the best-known year-round tourist attraction in the Pfalz, the *Derkemer Fass* (pronounced 'dare-k-ham'a fuss' – the Dürkheim Wine-Cask). On the fairground, under the shelter of tents large and small, incredible amounts of 'Worscht' and 'Woi' (pronounced 'voy' – wine) as well as other foods solid or liquid are consumed on row after row of wooden benches along row after row of tables. The *Fass*, a cask-shaped wooden structure which houses a restaurant that seats 450 visitors – or measured in cubic content would hold 1.700.000 liters of wine – is running over with people, too, during the fortnight of sustained and often boisterous celebration.

The *Fass* is still under family management, which stands to prove that spirited enterprise can net success even in these hard times. Over two million visitors from far and near filter through the entrance of the *Fass* per year.

One time the *Fass* literally resounded, with more than songs of wine, women and *Worscht* enthusiastically intonated by spontaneously formed choirs. The new chair-lift across the road was attracting attention to its own services up the mountain by blaring music so powerful that the vibrations were playing the *Fass* like an instrument. The whole of the wooden structure seemed to be humming along. Landlord, waiters and waitresses, and soon the guests, too, were complaining of excruciating headache. A change in the direction of the loudspeakers and the trouble was averted. Since, the *Fass* has never again played the 'devil's fiddle', and anyone with a headache must look around for a different explanation.

Throughout the year, fleets of tourist buses unleash their content on to the streets of *Derkem* so that the curious can discover the town for themselves. In turn the people of *Derkem* will go out to see these strangers.

This was precisely the reason why Seppl left his wife at home to tend to her home chores, while he made his rounds. Having had quite a bit to drink along the way, he decided on a round or two on the dancing floor. His dancing partner all picked out, he proceeded, not, however, until he had secured his proper place by putting a bottle of eau de toilette – a prize won at a tombola – on his seat. Returning from the dance floor he promptly sat down on top of the bottle and broke the glass.

The resulting discomfort sped up his decision to go home. At home, in front of the large dressing mirror in the hall, he lowered his trousers to inspect the damage. He then reached for the first-aid box to patch up the cuts, and finally retired most discreetly into the bedroom.

The following morning his wife shook him – not discreetly at all – out of his slumber. 'You crafty so-and-so!' she yelled. 'You were at it again last night, weren't you? And what about all those silly strips of plaster sticking all over the hall mirror . . . ?'

The famous *Derkem* gambling casino, by the way, is decorated with numerous and large wall mirrors.

Duwwag

pronounced 'do-vugg', to rhyme with 'zoo bug'. High German: Tabak. English: Tobacco.

An old legend reports:

It was after the Thirty Years' War in the Pfalz. The majority of villages and towns had been gutted and ravaged, the population reduced to but a quarter of its pre-war size. Not an inopportune time for the devil to introduce *Duwwag* to the region.

Disguised as a farmer he conspicuously busied himself with setting new *Duwwag* plants, when a local peasant walked by. Curious as all true Pfälzer are, the peasant couldn't help asking the strange labourer, what the name of this little green plant was.

'If you can guess it yourself by tomorrow, the field is all yours,' the devil replied, plucked a few leaves and rolled them into a cigar. Puffing away he added: 'Then, what you can't smoke yourself, you can sell to others for a profit.'

The peasant went home, and as the offer was too seductive, he couldn't find any peace. Finally he smeared tar all over himself, opened a bag full of eider downs and rolled around in the feathers. In no time he looked more like a goose than a human being.

Early the following morning he crept into the field with these unfamiliar plants. When the devil arrived and found this peculiar intruder, he angrily yelled: 'Silly bird, get out of my *Duwwag* field!'

Thus a Palatinate peasant learned the name and won a field of *Duwwag* from the devil himself.

Up to this day *Duwwag* is planted profitably in the Pfalz. Even though the number of factories producing cigarettes, cigars and pipe tobacco have actually declined, tobacco growing still provides the state with welcome revenue. And we can enjoy the colourful pictures during harvest time or when the leaves are drying in rustling garlands in special airy barns alongside strings of yellow corn cobs.

Traditional conditions within the tobacco manufacturing industry were hardly that pleasant. Women and girls made up the majority of the underpaid labour force. Then as now each cigar made from the best of tobaccos must be sealed with a 'kiss' – the only way of fitting the cover leaf to a smooth end.

The less expensive types of cigars, on the other hand, had a tendency to 'explode'. They came undone, losing all shape – but providing smoker and on-looker with many an occasion for laughter. A cigar, though, from the cheapest cut of *Duwwag* that would look like a broom made of twiglets, was to no-one's delight. Yet it was still better than one with a high percentage of paper used inside.

The old expression 'In de Palz geht de Peffenbacher Parrer mit de Peif in die Kerch' (In the Pfalz the parson of Pfeffenbach goes to church with his pipe) does not only make fun of the way the Palatinates refuse to pronounce the letter 'f' after 'p',* it also hints at the popularity of smoking *Duwwag* in the days before the awareness of a health risk had been stirred.

* (see also letter P – *Pälzer*)

Ebbes

pronounced 'eb-bes' to rhyme with 'menace'.
High German: Etwas. English: Something.

A strong pointer to the age of the word *ebbes* is the fact that besides in Pfälzer dialect it also still exists in Yiddish. Considering that Yiddish has kept numerous words alive of the medieval German once spoken in the Rhine valley, it may become clear that to say *ebbes* about the word *ebbes* is quite *ebbes*.

Ebbes makes thing smaller to befit the human dimension. For instance 'a bit' has become 'a little bit' as soon as you hear *ebbes* like 'ich hab *ebbes* "gesse" ' (pronounced '*ich* hub eb-bes guess-a' with the '*ich*' sounding like in the Scottish word 'n*ich*t' – I've eaten a little something).

The comparative of *ebbes* is *noch ebbes* (pronounced '*noch* eb-bes' as in the Scottish word 'l*och*' – something more). Accordingly *Helmut Metzger*, one of the better-known versifiers in the vernacular, gave two of his books the titles *Ebbes* (vol. 1) and *Noch ebbes* (vol. 2). He employs the word *ebbes* with the artistry of a master juggler.

'Of *ebbes* you can make *ebbes*', he muses. 'A young man should make sure that his bride has *ebbes*, knows *ebbes* and brings *ebbes* into the marriage (a dowry). When he has found such a girl, he has got *ebbes* to fill his heart and soul with joy – *ebbes* for the rest of his life.

The wedding may cost *ebbes* to show that the

families have *ebbes*. For you all know that the one who has *ebbes* usually gets *ebbes* more.

During their honeymoon travels the young couple see *ebbes*, experience *ebbes*, buy *ebbes* to bring *ebbes* home for their folks.'

And so on it goes, until the young wife expects *ebbes*. Then, 'if the baby cries, *ebbes* is wrong with him. If he is hungry, he is fed *ebbes*. If he doesn't stop crying, maybe his mother finds *ebbes* in his nappies . . . '

Whenever *Helmut Metzger* reads from his books anywhere in the Pfalz, he can be sure of applause. He and others like him write in the tradition of the late *Paul Münch*, the best-known of all those who have ever written in the Palatinate vernacular.

He boldly declared the Pfalz to be the centre of the earth:

> It's here that our globe is joined,
> here is the axle and its lubrication point.

In the wine country of the Pfalz there is no doubt as to the lubricant.

Erwed

pronounced 'er-ved' to rhyme with 'carrot(d)'. High German: Arbeit. English: Work, labour, a job.

To the Pfälzer a fundamental difference exists between the concept or immanent threat of *Erwed* and the actual trouble of having to work, though one is as bad as the other. Even semantically this becomes transparent in the popular maxim: 'Schaffe is ä *Erwed*!' (pronounced 'shuf-fa is a(y) er-ved' – working amounts to outright labour).

We looked up some learned books on the subject of Palatinate semantics and vocabularly. In *Der brauchtümliche Wortschatz im Überlieferungsbestand der Pfalz* (only one of the titles, and we spare you and us the translation) there is not one single reference to either *Erwed* or 'schaffe', which goes to show, what little rôle either play in the philosophy of the Pfälzer.

Well-known is a granny's advice: 'Child, don't study so hard, or when you're grown up you'll have to work too much.'

This Palatinate attitude toward *Erwed* stands in marked contrast to the one of the neighbouring Swabians, whose only purpose in life is said to be: 'to work, to save up, to build a house and then die.' Full of concern and an urgent warning in his voice, a Pfälzer will utter: 'He worked himself under the ground!'

To assume therefore that for every German alive the

greatest virtue lies in a diligent and exhaustive performance at work, is as silly as generalizations generally are. People work because they have to. Either because of need and necessity, or because of social terror. To the former the Pfälzer will submit, social terror they have a long tradition of disobeying.

Until the recent, at least occasional admission of vernacular language into the class room, the Palatinates were made to believe that High German was more acceptable, refined and noble than their own dialect. Hence, when they have a job, they say they have *Erwed*, if they are unemployed they use the High German term 'Arbeitslosigkeit' (pronounced 'are-bites-loh-zick-kite'). In light of the linguistic hierarchy it is clear to see which of the two they rank higher.

Far from being idlers, the Pfälzer do, however, regard themselves anatomically at a disadvantage, when it comes to the worst, to the threat of *Erwed* or 'schaffe'. How else would you interprete 'He only uses his feet to step out of the way of *Erwed*'? Fulfillment of their highest and most treasured dream would be a situation, where with *Erwed* or 'arbeitslos' they had 'nix to schaffe' (pronounced 'nix toe shuf-fa' – nothing to do).

And second best to this utopian bliss? Here's is a clue, given in a casual exchange between two Pfälzer passing one another on their bikes.

'Hi there, how?'

'Lousy. You?'

'Fine. The wife found herself *Erwed*!'

What a wealth of wisdom lies in such brevity!

Fissemadende

pronounced 'fizz-a-mud-end-a' to rhyme with 'fill an agenda'. High German: Fisimatente (in the plural only). English: Fuss, nonsense, playful pranks, tricks, fibs . . . and much more.

Fissemadende are nothing one would ask for. But in the face of any of the numerous varieties that fall under the general authority of the term, immediate comment is called for, either with an undertone of disapproval or with an amused smile. 'Mach kää *Fissemadende*!' (Don't make such fuss! or Stop that nonsense) you will hear everywhere in the Pfalz. The fuss-, fib- and fun-loving natives always appreciate playful and imaginative inventiveness, and so the use of the term is secured for centuries to come.

The most sophisticated explanation as to the root of *Fissemadende* can be found in a dictionary compiled by a Herr Kluge (whose name means 'clever' in German. No fib!).

In the 16th century, he writes, a lot of red tape was involved, when a scholar applied for his *visae patente (literae)* (his rightly deserved patent). So in mockery of the superfluous bureaucratic nonsense, the Latin phrase was adapted and adopted into the German and into the Palatinate language. Herr Kluge also cites another source, the term *visament* (unnecessary adornment), which is documented in the spelling *visimatent* as early as 1499.

The Pfälzer know better, as so often in similarly learned circumstances. They trace *Fissemadende* back to the time of the Napoleonic War, when the French had ordered a strict nightly curfew. During those hours the soldiers patrolled the streets, and whenever someone was caught outside, he or she was taken for interrogation. And what was the excuse given?

'Je viens de *visiter ma tante*!' (I've been visiting my aunty!)

The soldiers were supposed to believe this flimsy explanation. And as the mechanism of patriotic put-down of the brain power of foreign occupants prescribes, the Pfälzer proudly tell that they did.

Fissemadende come under noisy criticism, though, when they occur on the football field. All hell breaks loose, should a referee make *Fissemadende* and decide against the home team. 'You are too stupid to draw a full moon on paper!' is one of the less abusive shouts he may have to digest – with a good chuckle, we hope. Or a player does not – at least in the eyes of impatient fans – pass the ball quickly enough for a sure goal, dribbling along on an ego trip. What flowery language you might hear then. Particularly in the minor leagues or during friendly matches between village clubs. The barrage of hilariously picturesque comments, curses and swear words will delight any student of the Palatinate vernacular.

Big league football may have less colour, but *Fissemadende* it evokes, too. For the Pfälzer big league football, football itself, is identical with *F.C. Kaiserslautern*. A home game on the 'Betzeberg' makes any day into a high holiday for the fans. Donning red shirts and trousers they cheer for their 'Red Devils', the players of the one and only Kaiserslautern team.

Michael Bauer, a young guitarist and folk singer from the city, composed the saga of a fan in honour of the club, the 'Betzeberg Blues'. He describes the excitement and all the drama of the game, the drinking and the shouting. But then the *Fissemadende* begin to wear thin. The wooden crate on which he stands breaks under him. In the end, the winning team of *Bayern München* is beaten up by the home crowd.

The Monday morning hangover hurts, but when the newspaper comes, interest again is quickly aroused. '35000 spectators watched the game.' And the singer concludes with pride: 'One of them – was I.'

gell

pronounced 'guell' to rhyme with 'bell'. High German: gelt. English (approximately): isn't it? ain't it? Right?

You'd sooner extract a plausible answer from a Pfälzer to the question of why people keep breathing than to 'What do you mean by *gell*?'.

As far as the High German form *gelt* is concerned, it sounds a bit patronizing, affected, even presumptuous today. No matter that it has been around for a long time, since the 14th century in fact. In its original meaning it stood for 'May it be valid!' – as in the offer of a bet.

The popular form *gell*, or at times *gelle* (pronounced 'guell-a'), in use in the south and west of Germany, prominently and quite naturally ornaments the Pfälzer's speech. Just as the medieval English expressions 'yawp' and 'yaup' still flourish in the linguistic backwaters at a distance from the Queen's English, so do *gell* and *gelle* far from the formal German. In the Pfalz they come second in popularity, right after the all-time favourite *alla**.

Masked as an unassuming little interjection, *gell* is in reality more of a rhetorical trump-card thrown into the game at the very beginning or the very end. In either case, it may be thrown in with a bit of righteousness,

* (see also letter A – *Alla*)

may reassert authority temporarily lost, or may go along well with a twinkle in the speaker's eyes.

Of a person endowed with a healthy appetite and trying in vain to conceal the inevitable effects, you may hear in the Pfalz: '*Gell*, der glaabt aa, in ähm zu kläänе Kiddel werd der schlanker!' ('guell, de'a glahbt ah, in am tsoo clan-a kiddle verd de'a shlunker' – Look, he thinks by wearing a tight jacket, he'll slim down!)

Or referring to a lowly paid employee: '*Gell*, der hot vorne nix und hinne nix, des hot er awwer sicher!' ('guell, de'a hot forn-a nix (o)und hinn-a nix, dess hot e'a (l)over, *zich*er'† – He's got nothing before him, nothing behind him, but that he has for sure).

Someone for once short of a retort to a joke at his expense will have his defeat rubbed in by: 'Jetz hoscht doi Fett weg, *gell*?' (pronounced 'yets hosht doy fet veck, guell' – Now you've got yours, haven't you!)

A mother angry with her child will yell: 'Jetz langt's, *gell*!' (pronounced 'yets lungts, guell') meaning 'Now I've had enough, really!' In this case the warning better be heeded, or else . . .

Rarely will you find a mono-syllabic Pfälzer, and if you do, he probably is one provoked by having been told the obvious. Case in point, the following conversation between a Pfälzer couple:

'Can't you do something about this tap?' the wife asks her husband. 'It's dripping!'

'*Gell*!'

You can be sure that nothing will be done about the tap. For in the Palatinate those short in talk are long in doing, *gell*?!

† (as in Scots '*nicht*')

Grumbeer

pronounced 'groom-bare' to rhyme with 'book fair'. High German: Grundbirne, i.e. Kartoffel. English: Potato.

Just like in England, where one *Grumbeer* never comes alone either, *Grumbeere* (pronounced 'groom-bare-a' – potatoes) come chipped, boiled, mashed, dumpled or pancaked in the Pfalz, rarely in a jacket, though, but more frequently in a salad dish, instead.

Literally the term translates into 'ground pear', evoking visions of sweet fruits descending from the tree into fertile soil. Only such a poetic image in the eyes of the Pfälzer could do justice to their most beloved vegetable.

After its initial introduction into Europe, the *Grumbeer*, as the main staple food, soon was included in the traditional harvest customs. The harvesters, male or female, who fill the last sack of *Grumbeere* become the target for all sorts of teasing, all in good fun and in the happy relief that follows a hard job accomplished.

From early on, special sacks were tailored that would hold a hundred kilos (about 220 pounds) each. Strong backs were needed to carry such a load to a waiting cart. (And to this day the Pfalz is known for its strong men. Its wrestlers were winning World Championships as far back as 1912, when an athlete from Ludwigshafen won the title in Stockholm. In those days wrestlers would compete: no mats on the floor, on hard planks, starting from an upright position. Today it's the town of Schifferstadt that can be proud of its strong men and their sporting success.)

The Pfälzer and their *Grumbeere*! That almost has the same ring to it as saying: The Irish and their potatoes! In 1816/17 during a famine (not the first nor the last, certainly) people walked, drove or rode to the potato regions of Oggersheim, Ruchheim or the Sickinger Heights, to beg for a few pounds. Every war brought on the same, the last one not excluded.

In the city of Ludwigshafen, every stretch of parkland, every playground and each patch of green was converted into garden plots after the Second World War, mainly for growing *Grumbeere*.

'Quellde mit dubb-dubb' (pronounced 'kvell-de mit doobb-doobb') were the poor man's breakfast for a long time. Piping hot from the big pots, in which they had been carried to the vineyards or fields, the *Grumbeere* were dipped by the workers into salt to enhance the flavour.

Cooked with leeks, parsley and other vegetables, potatoes make a hearty *Grumbeere-Supp* ('groom-bare-a-zou(l)p') that the Palatinates love to top off with plum tart.* Elsewhere called *Puffer*, the *Grumbeere-Pannekuche* ('groom-bare-a-punn-a-coul(d)*ch*-a')† or pancakes can be adorned any way the individual taste prefers.

Grumbeere still find a use as home-made medicine. Boiled and mashed they are filled into a linen sack which then is placed on the part of the body, where it hurts. Or potato purée is given to a child that swallowed something pointed or sharp-edged.

Asked by a city-bred holidaymaker, why some pota-

* (see also under Q – *Quetsch*)
† (as in Scots 'lo*ch*')

toes have white and others pink blossoms, a Pfälzer farmer came up with a quick retort: 'One kind is for chips and the other for the mashed.'

A bad, watery *Grumbeer* is cruelly called 'Wasser-arsch', which, if you know the translation for Wasser, doesn't require any further explanation.

Handkees

pronounced 'hunt-caiss' to rhyme with 'front chaise'. High German: Handkäse. English: A medium soft cheese speciality.

By tradition, *Handkees* comes 'mit Musik' (pronounced 'moo-zeak' – with music). But any Wagnerian will be waiting in vain . . .

Handkees is more than just a laugh. It's quite a job to make. Each individual *Handkees* is padded and shaped from a heaped handful of curd cheese and placed on a wooden board. Covered with a piece of impeccable, white muslin to keep dust and the like off, the board then goes to a cool place. Daily checks are necessary so that any surplus liquid can be wiped off. Half-way through the maturing process the crumpet-shaped cheeses must be washed, with a piece of flannel soaked in wine – as the alcohol prevents the formation of fungi. Finally each *Handkees* is sprinkled with caraway seeds and kept in a crock, where it acquires its glassy texture.

The cheeses will also develop a strong smell, which tends to get stronger at room temperature. Then the *Handkees* will begin to run – for the connoisseur the welcome signal that it has reached the peak of its palatability.

But now, where does the music come in? When the waitress serves you a portion, does a band start playing 'Heil Dir im Siegerkranz' (to the tune of 'God Save the

Queen')? Hardly. 'Musik' refers to the garnishments that are served with the cheese, a little pretzel, a bit of paprika powder – and a generous helping of chopped onions dressed with vinegar and oil, and then the music can start!

Shops will sell you dairy produced *Handkees* neatly and tightly wrapped up in paper. Since each cheese is no more than just over half an inch thick they lend themselves to easy storage one stacked on top of the other. Three of them, therefore, can't stand to much of a height, and that is why a young school kid is often called a *Drei-Kees-hoch* (three cheeses high).

And someone lanky but boastful will have his self-deception cut to size, should he overhear the remark about him: 'He lifts a *Handkees* with one hand!'

Back to the 'Musik', i.e. the musical effects of *Handkees mit* . . . Once upon a time a man from Ludwigshafen was riding on a tram-car, when it happened. The lady next to him, from Mannheim, showed utter disgust. Not in the least concerned or embarrassed the Ludwigshafener turned to the lady and said to her for everyone around to hear: 'Don't be upset, Madam, that has happened to me once or twice before, too.'

Calling attention to the best-loved nourishments of the Pfälzer you will find a 'Wine Museum' in Speyer, a 'Beer Academy' in Ludwigshafen and a restaurant called *'Kees-Büro' (cheese office) in Bad* Dürkheim.

Horschemol

pronounced 'horsch-a-mall' to rhyme with 'bosh a Paul'. High German: Hör einmal! English: Listen! Listen, you!

Horschemol is one of the more ambivalent exclamations constantly used by the Pfälzer. Only a slight raising or lowering of the voice makes all the difference between an appeal for attention, a reproach, an urgent plea and many more.

'*Horschemol*! I want to tell you something!'

'Yes, what is it?'

'O . . . well, I forgot.'

'*Horschemol*! Do you want to take the mickey out of me or what?'

More often than not, *Horschemol* is just the opening of a conversation about anything. Addressing anyone in English by 'Listen, you!' is terribly rude. The Pfälzer, however, love the direct approach. They may on occasion concede to use the slightly more formal '*Horsche Se mol*!', but only if the addressee by bearing and reserve is a non-native, quite obviously.

As with numerous gestures and manners of speech, *Horschemol* or *Horsche Se mol* may well be traced back to the influence of nearby France, where 'écoute!' or 'écoutez!' are very familiar signals for the start of a friendly chat.

'*Horschemol*,' says a would-be intellectual to his companion, 'Did you know that Friedrich Schiller (a contemporary of Goethe and a writer of equal prestige) lived under an assumed name in Oggersheim, where he found cheaper quarters than in Mannheim? Even though his first drama 'Die Räuber' (The Robbers) had been a great success at the Mannheim National Theatre under the direction of Dalberg?'

'*Horschemol*! Do you think I'm stupid?'

'But no! And to think that this happened in 1782 . . . '

'Then tell me, who was this chap Schiller anyway?'

Finally, *Horschemol* will also stress a superior claim to fame or to being right, much like the English 'What do you want!'

Three boys on a playground are involved in an argument about the importance of their fathers, their social rank and their power.

'My Dad is with the fire brigade. If he wants to, your house will burn to the ground.' The first one proudly claims.

'Puh,' the second one responds, 'my Dad is a policeman. He can put you in prison any time!'

'*Horschemol*!' the last one triumphantly cries. 'My Dad is a doctor. If he operates on you, you will surely die!'

Iwwerdreiwe

pronounced 'ivver-drive-a' to rhyme with 'give a fiver'. High German: Übertreiben. English: To exaggerate.

To the Pfälzer no object, person, experience or occurrence is unworthy of or beyond exaggeration. In fact, to *iwwerdreiwe* amounts to nothing more than to describe anything in Pfälzische terms.

Possessing such an exuberant and imaginative vocabulary as he does, the Pfälzer feels compelled to use it true to the model of Oriental opulence. But rather than going for cheap superlatives, which require little intelligence, he will use composite terms nobody but he could think up or images of rare vivacity and precision.

Someone naked is 'puddelnaggisch' (pronounced 'pou(l)ddle-nuggish' – as naked as a trimmed poodle), someone not too bright is 'sau-bleed' (pronounced 'zow-blehd' – as stupid as a sow), and even a dead cat is 'mausedoot', which only sounds like 'dead as a mouse', but actually is a combination of 'dead' in German and a word for the same that goes back to either Latin or Hebrew – thus meaning 'double dead'.

To what extent the Pfälzer will go in order to *iwwerdreiwe* can be illustrated by the following episode:

During the French occupation of a village in the Pfalz, the commanding officer let it be known that he wished to talk matters over with 'the most intelligent man of the place.' Come next morning, not a male inhabitant of the village could be found. They all had fled during the night – each one of them considering himself 'the greatest of them all'.

In a Palatinate court, the judge once had a heart to heart talk with the unrepentant offender.

'So, as the plaintiff told us, you hit him over the head with a bottle of wine!'

'There is no need to *iwwerdreiwe*, Your Lordship,' the culprit defended himself. 'It was only a bottle of very light Moselle wine . . . '

This hair-raising farce was reported in the local press as 'the understatement of the year'.

In 1851 already, the Bishop of Speyer found occasion to issue a letter directing the priests in his diocese to refrain from *iwwerdreiwe* in meeting the public's demand for light music during weddings or christenings. Waltzes and marches should no longer be played on the church organ during these services.

With a people of such disposition there can be no end to anecdotes like this.

Quite a few of the Pfälzer exaggerations do have a tendency to debunk. 'She has a hair-do like a landslide' is certainly no compliment, but it gives a lively picture of a lady caught out in the rain. Or what about a wife, who during a marital spat put her balding husband in his place by saying: 'There is more hair on my leg than you've got on your head'?

The art of exaggeration is learned early in the Pfalz, even in children's rhymes:

Allah is gross, Allah is mächtig.
Allah hot ähn Hut uff von drei Meter sechzig.

Allah is great, Allah is fat.
Three metres round is the size of his hat.
(See also under A – *Alla*.)

Iwwerzwerch

pronounced 'iwer tsverch' to rhyme with 'quiver per (ish) ch (ch as in Scots 'nicht'). High German: Überzwerch. English: Transverse, crosswise, athwart, topsy-turvy. 'Zwerch' also has the same root as the German 'Zwerg' and its equivalent in English: 'dwarf'.

Not altogether unexpectedly, some things in the Pfalz are *iwwerzwerch*, quite out of the ordinary. Anyone venturing across the demarcation lines of traditional logic is accordingly said to be talking *iwwerzwerch*. And you can blame it on the care-free temperament of the Palatinates or on their favourite beverage, amply poured whenever, wherever, should you see someone wearing a jacket *iwwerzwerch* on occasion, with the lining inside out.

Nothing, however, sounds more *iwwerzwerch* than the officially documented existence of *Zwerge* within the boundary of the Pfalz, at least until the year 1969. Who else but dwarfs would organize themselves in *Zwerggemeinden* (dwarf communities) of never more than 300 souls; and perhaps in those communal units we have finally found the last traces of the kith and kin of Cornish and Celtic fairy creatures? They also attended *Zwergschulen* (dwarf schools).

Yet with the year 1969 and changing social conditions came the administrative reforms under the then Prime

Minister of the Rhineland-Palatinate, Herr Dr. Helmuth Kohl. (Dr. Kohl is a native of Ludwigshafen – see also under letter O – *Onilinfawwrik* – and serves at present as chairman of the Christian Democratic Party, or CDU.) Under Dr. Kohl's democratic guidance the *Zwerggemeinden* were joined into larger units, into a kind of super dwarf communities (i.e. *Iwwerzwerch-Gemeinden* in the vernacular), a measure which saved the state budget and in the last instance the tax payers millions of Deutschmarks.

Not since Napoleonic times had reforms of such consequence been introduced into and ratified by the government of a Land. And this only because no-one since Napoleon had dared to subject the complex structure of state administration to such a revolutionary change, until the one instigated by a political party usually thought of as conservative.

Traditions take hold slowly and are hard to uproot. Except when you are dealing with the *iwwerzwerche* Pfälzer – and Dr. Kohl, being one of them, could count on that. Legislation for the *Iwwerzwerch-Gemeinden* (not quite their proper name, of course) was put into practice by the Landtag in Mainz (the Rhineland-Palatinate state parliament).

Given a few jerks and hitches here and there, the reforms have worked admirably and have found many admirers, though few imitators elsewhere.

Not long ago, I overheard a neighbour proudly commenting about her son's oratory talents – and he almost seemed to be drowning out an imaginary election meeting: 'This child talks so *iwwerzwerch*, he is sure to make his way into the Landtag . . . '

That was meant to be a compliment. May-be it was. Given a few jerks and hitches the child will probably reform into a genuine *Iwwerzwerg*, vocal and democratic as the Pfälzer tend to be by tradition.

Judde

pronounced 'youdd-a' to rhyme with 'could ye'. High German: Juden. English: Jews.

Even in a light-hearted book of fun there ought to be a page or two where amusement ceases: to commemorate the victims of unspeakable cruelties and murderous crimes committed against German Jewry by the Nazis.

Today the Pfälzer themselves are mostly unaware of how close the relationship was with which they lived side by side with the *Judde* of the region. Their very language, however, furnishes us with a memorial tablet of an earlier symbiosis. In 1802 already a traveller through the Pfalz observed: 'The Germans here have a peculiar dialect not unlike the Jewish idiom in Poland . . .'

What he failed to point out was that the presence of Jewish families in the Pfalz is well documented for as far back as Roman times. Already then, Jews had built their temples and ritual bath houses, remnants of which can still be found.

During the Middle Ages the communities of *Speyer, Worms* and *Landau* counted *Judde* among their traders as well as peasants, even though the Jewish population was living under precarious conditions not only in and around the age of the crusades. Standards of learning were high, and the adaption and adoption of words and phrases from the medieval German and from Hebrew were mutual and quite customary. Yiddish owed as much to Pfälzisch as the popular language of the Pfalz owes to Yiddish.

A recently published dictionary [Kurt Bräutigam, *So werd bei uns geredd* (Mannheim, 1979) – This is the way we talk] gives a sizeable selection of vernacular expressions and produces ample evidence of linguistic linkages. The special social terms under which the *Judde* were forced to live throughout, are reflected in the number of expressions reacting against numerous types of degradation. These are still in use in the Pfalz and considered amusing today, their roots forgotten by all but a few linguists. There is little consolation in the fact that under the Kaisers and during the first German republic Jewish communities began to prosper. That ended all too sudden and with gruesome finality in 1940.

The childhood reminiscences of *Hermann Sinsheimer*, who was born in *Freinsheim*, offer us a glimpse of the conditions after the turn of the last century. He describes how the youngsters of his village were alarmed by the arrival 'of a dark-looking stranger using a foreign idiom, carrying a knapsack and not being very clean.' Nobody explained to them that the stranger was, as it turned out, a Russian *Judd*, who lost his family in a czarist pogrom and was begging his way to the only haven of hope for him – to what was then Palestine.

Hermann Sinsheimer fled the Nazis and came to England, where he died in 1950. His name is mentioned here to stand for many thousands of Jews from the Pfalz.

It takes people of sensitivity and understanding to appreciate the full meaning of the *Judde* joke: 'The knife in my back only hurts, when I am laughing.'

Kunschd

pronounced 'counshd' to rhyme with 'lunched' if the vowel is pronounced as in 'push'. High German: Kunst. English: Art.

Scholars and critics discussing the whole spectrum of the arts in the Pfalz all come to the same conclusion – while *Kunschd* does exist there, the artists who produced it tended to emigrate, involuntarily or of their own accord.

During the peak of their power and influence, the mightiest sponsors of *Kunschd* throughout the ages, first the Church and later the Courts, did create centres for the arts in the Palatinate. *Zweibrücken* was one, *Mannheim* another. But wars and the ever changing pattern of religious and political allegiance forced upon the region allowed no consistency. The residence of the Bavarian kings, *Munich*, proved far more attractive, as it was here that the visual arts in particular found patronage, and sculptors and painters employment. Altogether, the Pfalz never became the proper place for discussions on *Kunschd*, for artistic competition or display.

In a debate about the 'Meaning' of art, a Pfälzer is reported to have quipped: 'Was soll *Kunschd*? *Kunschd* mir fünf Mark pumpe?' (What about art? Art thou willing to lend me five Marks?)

It would be unfair to let the argument stand here: *Ludwigshafen* built an impressive new museum around the collection of a Mr. Hack. *Kaiserslautern* houses the Pfalz Gallery. Schloss Ludwigshöhe near *Edenkoben* offers a permanent exhibition of the works of *Max Slevogt*. Again, *Kaiserslautern* has a theatre with its own ensemble, while *Ludwigshafen* provides touring companies with a place to perform, the Pfalzbau-Theatre. (Thereby avoiding competition with *Mannheim* and its National Theatre just across the river; which is also called the 'Schiller Stage' in reverence to *Friedrich Schiller*, whose early dramas were first presented to the public there during the latter part of the 18th century.)

A general disinterest in *Kunschd* prevails side by side with a certain snobbery among art patrons. They rather travel outside the Pfalz than organize regional activities. Perhaps it was this kind of attitude that caused a painter of the stature of *Hans Purrmann* to make his home in Italy and Switzerland, where he died in 1966.

On the other hand, the Pfälzer love to play host to famous musicians, both serious and light, who make their appearances from *Landau* in the south to *Ludwigshafen* and *Worms* in the northern part of the Pfalz. They would have booked the *Beatles* regardless of the cost! Their tolerance in *Kunschd* being as broad as it is.

One attitude to *Kunschd* is hard to find – I am thinking of respect for the individual achievement. The Pfälzer will sooner get 'pally' with the local artists than show interest and sensitivity for their personal artistic style or their vision. Those trying to pursue their work in the Pfalz find this rather crippling.

Outside the Kunsthalle of *Mannheim* (the municipal Art Museum) a bronze sculpture depicts a life-size lioness with a long stretched-out tail. If the looker-on cares to inspect the sculpture at close range, he will detect traces of soldering on the tail of the beast.

One dark night, scrap metal thieves amputated the lioness by sawing off its tail. Later it was carefully replaced. This soldered bronze tail seems the symbol for the ongoing struggle between Pfälzer utilitarianism and *Kunschd*.

Leeweherz

pronounced 'lave-a-herrts' to rhyme with 'gayer shirts' (as pronounced in Inverness). High German: Löwenherz. English: (King Richard I) Lion-Heart.

It must have been a fine piece of cunning and conniving: the Pfälzer taking over the *Leeweherz* from his Austrian captors to lock him away in the keep of the *Trifels*. Such is said to have happened to the king on his return from Syria and the Third Crusade.

If it is true (and sources cast some doubt on the factuality), *Leeweherz* was certainly not left thirsty. They still make excellent wines from the grapes growing in the South Pfalz, where the *Trifels* (pronounced 'tree fells') proudly crowns a sizeable rock near *Annweiler*. Richard the Lion-Heart must have enjoyed every goblet filled with the delicious liquid.

Meanwhile the English tax collectors of the day must have sweated to gather his ransom. For two years the king endured imprisonment in the Pfalz until – according to a Palatinate legend – the French troubadour Blondel freed him. (The same Blondel, who is said to have discovered his master, when still in Austrian hands, by singing outside his dungeon and hearing a familiar tune in response from the king.) However romantic the story of Blondel's freeing the king may sound, 150,000 Marks in silver and the fulfillment of other conditions set by Emperor Henry VI amount to a much more reasonable cause for *Leeweherz'* release in 1194.

Josef Victor von Scheffel, a poet from neighbouring Badenia, took the fate of Richard to heart and in 1881 published his version of an Old French Chanson de Geste 'König Richard von England.' Besides a touch of very popular sentimentality the poem reveals some deep insight into human nature:

> No friend nor cousin is prepared to shed
> a tear for him who is imprisoned or is dead.
> When begged for gold and silver, all they offer
> is poverty out of an empty coffer.

Not far from the village of *Schweigen* and the *Weintor* (a gateway marking the southern end of the famous *Weinstrasse* that leads up to Bockenheim to the north) the *Trifels* rises up. Anyone driving by is welcome to see for himself, how strong and impenetrable the castle must have been, where *Leeweherz* was held; where also the Crown Jewels of the medieval German Empire were stacked away for quite some time.

Lui

pronounced 'loo-ey' to rhyme with 'screwy!'
High German: Ludwig. English: Louis.

Colloquially the Pfälzer may refer to someone not too well off, but trying to gloss over his miserable state of affairs, as a *'Pomade-Lui'* (or one who uses excessive amounts of hair grease). The derogatory implication of the name, which is directly derived from the French *Louis*, points at once to the somewhat checkered relationship between the Pfalz and France.

History is full of instances, when the Pfalz was occupied by, interfered with or under the influence of the French. During the periods of religious intolerance, the Pfalz saw the large-scale immigration of French Huguenots, who settled permanently. After the marriage of Princess *Liselotte von der Pfalz* to the brother of *Louis XIV*, alleged dowry claims were given as the reason for numerous raids into the Pfalz ordered by the French crown from the year 1688 onward. *Mannheim* and *Heidelberg* were burnt down in their course. The fortress of *Landau* was under French rule for 150 years.

Is it any wonder, therefore, that French names and expressions found their way into the Pfälzische vernacular, in spite of many a painful memory? For long periods *Louis* (*Lui*) *Jean* or *Babette* (*Bawett* in the Pfalz) were most popular first names. The peculiar form 'seller' (fem. 'selli' – pronounced 'zeller' and 'zelley') for 'this' and 'that' person can only be understood, when one knows their origin in the French 'ce lui' and 'celle-là'.

From November 1918 until 30 June 1930 the Pfalz remained under occupation by the French 8th Army, in accordance with the armistice agreement after World War I. A century earlier, too, the region had been taken over by France until the fall of Napoleon – which, according to reports, was seen by the native population with regret. The event, though, brought the Pfalz again under Bavarian rule, first under King Max-Joseph, subsequently under *Ludwig I*. And with it came the change from *Lui* to the more respectfully sounding *Ludwig*.

Innumerable streets, public squares and churches have carried the monarch's name since. (See also under K – *Kunschd* and the reference to the castle *Ludwigshöhe*) But the most important locality named after the Bavarian *Ludwig* is the largest city in the Pfalz, *Ludwigshafen*, founded during his reign. (Not to be mistaken for a much smaller town of the same name on Lake Constance.)

Until then, the place, where this industrial city is situated now, was nothing but a farming area with a fortified bridge-head across the Rhine from *Mannheim*. The natural bay that had been washed out by high waters of the River Rhine was built into a harbour in 1845. 1847: cargo transport to and from this harbour was made possible by way of newly constructed railway lines. 1865: the first factory buildings were erected for the production of chemical dyes and soda. (See under O – *Onilin*) Ever since, *Ludwigshafen* has continued to grow, at 'American speed' quite often, increasing its population and spreading outward into every direction.

By coincidence, the city has for some time now been administered by a lord mayor, whose name, very appropriately, is Werner *Ludwig*. Little surprise that the new City Centre, a multi-storey glass-tower housing the municipal administration, is called *Ludwigsburg*, and the Lord Mayor's office up on the highest floor *Ludwigshöhe*. Nothing is easier than to draw Dr. *Ludwig* into the genuine Pfälzer vernacular.

He even knows by heart some of the verses from the very amusing *Kinnersprich vum Ludewig* (pronounced 'kinner-shp*rich* foom lude-a-v*ich*' – *ich* as in Scots 'n*icht*') a collection of children's verses in dialect by the late *Ludwig Hartmann*, first published in 1922.

Westerly winds prevailing, the smells of *Ludwigshafen*, that is of the chemical works, tend to descend over the city across the Rhine. Cause enough for the people of *Mannheim* to translate *Ludwigshafen (Ludwig's* harbour) jokingly into the French 'Boîte-chambre de *Louis*' (Louis' chamber pot). Luckily, recent legislation stipulates that the various chemical factories, once discharging their smelly affluence into the air and into the waters of the Rhine, must install ever more and better filters today.

Mensch Maier

pronounced 'mensh mire' to rhyme with 'bench hire'. An exclamation used in the Pfalz, with 'Maier' also spelled 'Meier', 'Mayer' or 'Meyer'.

Who in the world was this *Mensch* (man, human being) by the name of *Maier*? He is always called upon, when something strikes the Pfälzer as astonishing or strange. Nobody seems to know the answer. The expression might be of Saxon origin, where 'Meier' referred to a dairy-farmer or an estate manager.

Anyway, here is the story of a certain Schorsch ('shorsh' – George) from *Pirmasens* in the Pfalz. Schorsch, because of his build, had been selected to serve as one of Frederic the Great's 'Tall Guys' in Potsdam, Prussia. While on duty, he had set his bayonet against the sentry-box and was busy preparing a sandwich with Pfälzer *Handkees*. An old gentleman approached, walking with a cane.

Not taking any notice, Schorsch went on with the business at hand. The following conversation ensued:

Gent.: 'For how long has He been in service?'

Schorsch: 'Have a guess!'

Gent., suppressing some anger: 'Two years?'

Schorsch: 'Wrong.'

Gent.: 'One year?'

Schorsch: 'Wrong again.'

Gent.: 'Half a year?'

Schorsch: 'Still wrong.'
Gent.: 'A quarter of a year, then?'
Schorsch: 'Yep, you got it!'
The old gentleman, hiding his amusement, walked on.
On second thought, Schorsch called him back.
Schorsch: '*Horschemol,*' (see also under letter H), 'who are you, going around nosy like that?'
Gent.: 'Have a guess!'
Schorsch: 'A serjeant?'
Gent.: 'Wrong.'
Schorsch: 'A lieutenant?'
Gent.: 'Wrong.'
Schorsch: 'A captain?'
Gent.: 'Wrong again.'
Schorsch: 'You don't mean to say – a general?'
Gent.: 'Still higher.'
Schorsch: 'Well, the king of Prussia, then?'
To which Frederic, who loved to walk around disguised as a civilian, replied: 'Yep, you guessed it . . . '
Schorsch, excited,: '*Mensch Maier* – Here, hold my sandwich for a second. For Your Majesty I have to stand at attention!'

If anything, this unperturbed use of *Mensch Maier* in front of the king shows a truly Pfälzer attitude toward those of high rank. Even the Bavarian monarch, *Ludwig* (see under letter L – *Lui*) sighed about the liberal way in which his subjects in the Pfalz dealt with his civil servants, even with himself – in vast contrast to the deference displayed by the Bavarian population.

Said monarch, once on a stag hunt in the Pfalz, had to disappear behind a tree. On his return, to everybody's embarrassment, his flies were still unbuttoned. The diplomats in the party least knew how to break the news to His Majesty. It took a Pfälzer game-keeper to save the situation.

Unbuttoning his own flies, he stepped up to the king and said: '*Mensch Maier*, Your Majesty – Look at us. Hadn't we better button up our trousers?'

The king complied, and the hunt went on.

Närrischkeit

pronounced 'narrish-kite' to rhyme with 'parish fight'. High German: Narretei, Närrischkeit. English: Foolishness, folly.

To be or not to be a fool, is no question during the fools' season that officially starts on the eleventh day of the eleventh month at eleven minutes after eleven o'clock. From then on – with the exception of the Advent and Christmas period – until Ash Wednesday, Prince *Karneval* holds the Pfalz under his reign. (Even though scholars cannot settle the question, whether *Karneval* comes from *carne-vale* – 'hurrah for meat', from *carne levare* – 'leaving out meat' or from *carrus navalis* – 'festive float'.)

Närrischkeit comes so natural to the Pfälzer that they cannot get enough of it. And accordingly they drew on various customs from different historical roots to fill their fools' season: with masquerading, noisy rattles, showers of confetti and caramels, music, dancing, dining and wining and much, much more. It's the time, when the fool's motto: 'Wine makes the weak strong and the strong weak' is tested most democratically –by everyone.

Linking arms with your neighbours to *schunkeln* ('shoonclen' – to sway back and forth) you will soon feel part of the free, equal and fraternal community celebrating *Närrischkeit*. It may break out spontaneously in the streets or climax during the carnivalistic pomp that is staged in large halls and small pubs alike. The *Fools Guard* appear in mock soldier costumes reminiscent of the Napoleonic army. Their mascotte, pretty *Funkenmariechen* (little sparkling Mary) delights with her dance solo. Pageantry and buffonery everywhere.

Carnival in the Pfalz, and better known there under the name of *Fasnacht* (night before the fasting period), has retained features quite unspoilt by commercialism. The performers on stage are almost all amateurs, the singers, the dancers as well as the *Büttenredner* (speakers from the vat). Whoever wears a fool's cap or enters the vat has the fool's freedom of speech. The wittier and more satirical these contributions in prose or verse, the greater the appreciation from the audience.

'What is the difference between a grandfather clock and Germany?' one Pfälzische *Büttenredner* is reported to have asked his partner back in 1849. The reply: 'The clock beats the hours, but Germany is beaten for her hours of freedom.' Wisdom under a fool's cap.

Nowadays, *Närrischkeit* during the Fasnacht season is mainly an outlet for people's desire to dress up, to poke fun at one another and to shed the restrictions of everyday life.

Under the Nazis there existed neither the freedom nor the occasion for clubs to organize carnivalistic activities. Only after the Second World War did they start to flourish again. As a lot of organization goes even into *Närrischkeit* in the Pfalz, and many a club stages ten and more *Narrensitzungen* (fools sessions) per season, the administrative body of such a club is set up along the lines of a government. The *Elferrat* (council of eleven) consists of: President, Vice-President, Foreign Minister, Purser (to collect fines from fools overstepping the rules!) and, of course, Chamberlain to pour the wine from a large decanter. Large clubs may have several *Elferräte* and a *Senate*, as upper house. Each club signs under a special name, usually recalling a funny story or event of the locality.

As participation is of great social value and strictly voluntary, ministers, mayors, business men and professionals make it a point of honour to subscribe and give their time and support for the entertainment of children and old-age pensioners as well.

Year by year, newly created *Karnevalsschlager* (pop songs for the occasion) compete for popularity and reveal quite a bit about the mood of the times.

1912: 'Es war einmal ein treuer Husar' (There once was a loyal hussar).

1922: 'Wir versaufen unser Oma ihr klein Häuschen' (We are converting Grandma's little house into alcohol).

1938: 'Kornblumenblau' (Corn-flower-blue is the sky along the beautiful Rhine).

1949: 'Wer soll das bezahlen' (Who has enough money to pay for it).

1950: 'Auf Wiedersehn' (Till we meet again): etc.

The most characteristic tune for *Närrischkeit* in the Pfalz is an old one on 'Ritz-am-Bää', a bowdlerization of the name of the French general Richard Pierre. He committed the unforgivable mistake of banning Fasnacht revelries. The Pfälzer marched to his residence singing this song in his 'praise' at the top of their voices – and he reversed his decision. Fools win their wars without bloodshed.

Unorganized *Närrischkeit* with a good deal of individual courage was displayed at times during the Nazi Regime, too.

In 1937 a fishmonger in Mannheim drew attention to his merchandise by yelling (in reference to Reichsmarschall Hermann Goering, Hitler's second in command, known for his weight problem):

'Buy my herring – fat like Hermann Goering!'

No sooner did the Gestapo (the secret police) get wind of it than the man was bundled into a car and taken to the police station. There he was intimidated and kept locked up in a cell for a night as a warning.

On the next market day, he was selling fish again. But he had learned his lesson. So he yelled:

'Buy my herring – fat like . . . last week's . . .'

Onilinfawwrik

pronounced 'onney-lean-fuvrick' to rhyme with 'Bonnie clean Pa's brick'. High German: Badische Anilin- *& Sodafabrik (BASF Ludwigshafen). English: BASF Chemical Works.*

As the late Dr. Ernst Johann rightly observed: The universe is constructed according to the principle laid down in an equation by Albert Einstein. While Ludwigshafen, the largest city in the Pfalz was founded on the basis of the formula $C_6H_5NH_2$.

The formula, for a substance first called 'Mauvin' and later 'Anilin', extracted from coal-tar, had been discovered by A.W. Hofmann. An English chemist, William Perkin, first succeeded in making dyes from *Anilin,* sold his patent to a German, who, with the help of other businessmen and scientists, established the BASF.

Originally the Badische Anilin- & Sodafabrik was registered in Mannheim on the other bank of the Rhine, in Badenia. Yet environmental considerations caused the Mannheim municipal council to withhold permission for the construction of such a 'witch's cauldron'. In 1865 the factory was started across the river in a place then under Bavarian jurisdiction, on the Palatinate side. The name 'Badische', however, has stuck to this day.

More or less around the first brick buildings of the *Onilinfawwrik,* the township of Ludwigshafen developed. With continental westerly winds prevailing, Mannheim profits from the foresight of a century ago by getting much of the industrial fumes and stench from neighbouring Ludwigshafen today. And the Pfalz receives all the revenue from a turnover that runs into tens of billions of Deutschmarks per year.

From the earliest days of the *Fawwrik* onward, the need for highly skilled technical staff, researchers and craftsmen to develop and put into practice ever advancing technological systems grew consistently. With the influx of engineers, technicians, kiln operators, carpenters and workers of various skills, Ludwigshafen had to satisfy an ever increasing demand for factory space, housing, health care, transport etc. etc.

The young community in consequence underwent plenty of strife and struggle in its time. Worse, it had to pay for progress and scientific advancement dearly, suffering severe loss of human lives during the two tremendous explosions of 1921 and 1948, in particular.

On the other hand, the *Onilinfawwrik* takes second place only to Mother Nature in feeding and providing for the population of Ludwigshafen. It also leads in the campaign against abusive smoking – and no cigarette may be lit after entering any one of the factory gates.

Today the plant has acquired the character of a city within a city. The number of patents developed in its laboratories and on its work-benches test the range of imagination. Textile and plastic industries owe much to the BASF, so does agriculture for the production of pest controls and fertilizers. In 1936 Sir Thomas Beecham took the London Philharmonic Orchestra to Ludwigshafen even, to try out and record a concert on BASF tapes, invented just two years beforehand.

To be a native of Ludwigshafen means to be closely familiar with facts of chemistry, the natural sciences and all the technology that goes along.

A senior citizen, Mrs. Barbara Schmitt of Oppau, was

asked to reveal the secret of her old age – an age of well over a hundred years. 'Mother Schmitt,' they asked her, 'how did you do it?' To which she is supposed to have replied:

'By a good daily diet from the *Onilinfawwrik*. In the morning I inhale the fishy smell of aethylamine, in the afternoon I breathe in the odour of violets, a side product of vitamin A production, and at night I take in a deep breath of SO_2.'

The emission of SO_2 or sulphor dioxide, is well under control these days. Senior citizens even complain that their lives are shortened, now that the *Onilinfawwrik* no longer supplies the beneficial odours. Well, our modern life is known to destroy all the old values . . .

Pälzer

pronounced 'pal-tser' to rhyme with 'seltzer'. High German: Pfälzer. English: Someone from the Palatinate or of Palatinate origin.

Any attempt at defining who is and what makes a *Pälzer*, will get hopelessly entangled in the absurdities of life. The very part of the world a *Pälzer* will call home seems open-ended, generating and absorbing influences. The river Nahe to the north constitutes but a weak barrier and has allowed linguistic similarities to persist between the people living in the mountains of the Hunsruck and those in the Pfalz. To the south, in the Alsace, many customs, expressions and characteristics also point to a relationship as close as the one to the Lorraine in the west and to the Alemanic neighbours on the right bank of the Rhine to Karlsruhe and beyond.

From whatever angle you may wish to look at them, the *Pälzer* turn out to be a regular mish-mash.

One fact alone has been firmly established. *Pälzisch* belongs to the family of languages known as *Rhine-Frankish*. Yet wave after wave of immigration of Huguenots, Walloons, Swiss, Jews and others left their mark on the *Pälzer* and their language. After the 30-Years War it was the Croatians and the Spaniards that settled in the heavily depopulated area. Add the French, and in more recent years the Italians, Greeks, Yugoslavs, Turks and others as well, who live there now – and it becomes clear that all these good folks thrown together must produce a special kind of brew.

Phonetically there are certain rules of thumb by which a *Pälzer* can be recognized, wherever you may encounter him. Even as far afield as America, where today there live a greater number of *Pälzer* and their descendants than in the *Palz* itself. And all of them will swallow the letter *f* after *p* (saying *Palz* for *Pfalz* and *Pälzer* for *Pfälzer*). High German *p* and *t* – with a few exceptions – are pronounced as *b* and *d*. This softening of the consonants also spills over to the letter *k* which tends to sound like g.

For that reason one may rightfully conclude that the *Pälzer*, as a matter of policy and diplomacy, is keenly interested in rounding off any corner. So much so that his *b* is mollified into a *w* (pronounced 'v') as in his favourite and firmly held principle 'Siwwe ä gradi Zahl soi losse' (High German: Sieben eine gerade Zahl sein lassen. English: To count seven among the even numbers), his appeal for tolerance.

One of the greatest diplomats the *Palz* ever produced, was Paul Thiry von Holbach, who contributed to Diderot's famous encyclopaedia and carried out diplomatic missions at the Russian Court in St. Petersburg on behalf of the French Crown. Joachim Johann Becher (1630-1682) was granted his patent in chemistry not in his native *Palz*, but in England – with the help of another *Pälzer*, Prince Ruprecht, son of the Winter Queen. Thomas Nast, yet another *Pälzer* and a fine cartoonist, fought with his crayon on President Lincoln's side in the American Civil War. The Hollerith – system, which is at the basis of our punch-card boom, was deviced by yet one more. The *Pälzer* Hugo Ball promoted Dadaism in Switzerland, the philosopher Ernst Bloch from Ludwigshafen proclaimed his 'Principle of Hope' while in exile in North America, and we chose England as the spot, where we'd rather cure any head cold that might catch us. In all, it has become most obvious that the *Palz* is a truly international affair.

In the Kasba of Algiers two *Pälzer* didn't trust their ears, when an Arab trader invited them into his bazaar with the words: 'Kummt roi – Summerschluss-Verkaaf' (*Pälzer* vernacular for 'Come in – summer sale!'). Obviously the North African must have worked for a time for the BASF (see also under O – *Onilinfawwrik*).

As all collective nouns, *Pälzer* describes a fiction with many aspects of reality. And the most real aspect of the *Pälzer* is the one closest to fiction: His principle of communicating with in- and outsiders in the knowledge that 'minnanner redde is besser als uffenanner schiesse', meaning: 'to talk with one another is better than to shoot at each other.'

Quatsch

pronounced 'kvutsch' to rhyme with 'touch'. High German: Quatsch, Unsinn. English: Nonsense, silliness.

A jocular song written in the thirties gives a good indication as to the whereabouts of the cradle of *Quatsch*, a word in use as much in the Pfalz as anywhere else in Germany. The verses go:

Du bist verrückt mein Kind,
Du musst nach Berlin.
Wo die Verrückten sind,
da gehörst du hin.

You are all mad, my love,
To Berlin with you.
Where all the madmen are,
You belong there, too.

Other than verbal, practical *Quatsch* is not necessarily bad either. Much depends on the prevailing mood, for instance the patience of adults for children, should they glue a coin to the pavement or fasten a purse on a long string, only to pull it away, when someone bends down to pick it up. These are considered pranks harmless enough, *Quatsch* for sure. Yet ever so often 'Mach keinen *Quatsch*!' (Don't be silly!) is used in defence against an inherent threat and spoken with a rather serious face. Almost as if the Southerner suddenly found himself confronted with the Berliners' notorious talent for aggression and readiness to pick a fight, however jocular. As if that aggression had travelled along with the word *Quatsch* from Berlin and the north of Germany and had gained access into the Pfalz, too.

Quatsch was first recorded in the form of *quat* (meaning 'evil' or 'bad') in 1573. Later the meaning changed, but even that wasn't enough for the Pfälzer. He had to top it all off. Hyperbolic as his manner of speech (and thinking) is his use of the term: '*Quatsch* mit Sauce!' he will mutter, 'Nonsense plus gravy'.

Pälzer Quatsch can come with laconic undertones, as in the case of one Peter Schäfer from Mannheim, both originator as well as subject of all sorts of witty anecdotes and *Quatsch* stories. Blume-Peter he was called, as he sold flowers for a living, a midget, heftily built and slightly retarded. It was the time, when poor social conditions were accompanied by squalor, lack of hygiene and their consequences.

Blume-Peter was enjoying a lull in the sun at a street corner, his flower basket beside him. Lost in day dreams, he was scratching his head and with such relish that a well-to-do passer-by couldn't suppress the remark:

'Hunting them, Peter?'

'Not really,' Peter replied without interrupting his activities, 'I take them as they come . . . '

The Pfälzer love this sort of verbal *Quatsch* no end. And they find themselves in good company among the Anglo-Saxons and Celts, the Slavs, Africans and Arabs, all known for their own types of *Quatsch* generators.

'Can you see across the river the chestnut tree there, next to the red roofed house?'

'Sure I can.'

'And the crow that settled on the top branch?'

'I can see that, too.'

'And that the bird is blind on its left eye?'
'That I can't see, but I thought as much.'
'How so?'
'Because it is wearing glasses, stupid . . .'
Pfälzer and Kurpfälzer alike are so fond of this Blume-Peter character, they even erected a life-size bronze statue in his honour, right in the centre of Mannheim. Where else would a simple man like he be so lovingly remembered?

Quedsch

pronounced 'kvedsch' to rhyme with 'pledge'. High German: Zwetschge. English: The blue (Continental) plum.

The *Quedsch* is a prune in adolescence. What then, would you say does the Pfälzer mean, when he calls a woman 'aldi *Quedsch*' (old *Quedsch*)?

While the Latin 'prunus domestica' became 'Pflaume' (plum) in most parts of North and East Germany, the southern and western dialects absorbed the sound of 'domestica' or of the North Italian 'davascena' (from Damascus – where the fruit originated) into 'Zwetschge' or 'Quetsche', and the Pfälzer call it *Quedsch*.

In August and September the fruit is shaken from the trees and gathered. That is the signal for the Pfälzer Hausfrau to bring out her baking tins the size of cart wheels or bath towels. It's time to bake *Quedsche-Kuche* (plum cake or tart). The more *Quedsche* ('kvedsh-a' for the plural) she manages to stack on the tart, de-stoned and halved and set upright into the dough, the greater her reputation as a baker. *Quedsche-Kuche* is served in the afternoon with coffee, or strange as it may sound, as a main course together with potato soup. It's the sweet and salty, the soft and crusty that make it into a delicious meal.

Someone who is trying to make a big impression by super refined table manners offers him- or herself automatically as a target for ridicule to the down-to-earth and unpretentious Pfälzer. 'They even dip their *Quedsche-Kuche* into their coffee.' Nice mess this is!

From *Quedsche* the famous *Quedsche-Schnaps* is distilled, too. (It is known in neighbouring Alsace simply as *Quedsch*, in the Black Forest as *Quedsche-Wasser* and in the Balkans as *Slivovicz*, with a slight difference in taste among all of these.) To the Pfälzer the difference in flavour has another reason. He prefers the one without the label that reads: 'Duty paid!'

According to recipes handed down from generation to generation the scrumptious plum jam called *Latwerch* or *Quedsche-Muus* (pronounced 'kvetsh-a-moose') is concocted. Though *Latwerch* (High German: Latwerge) used to be the collective name for all kinds of medicinal remedies, preferably of the purgative sort, the sweet jam of the same name is a different matter altogether. *Quedsche-Muus* or *Latwerch* is boiled down to a particularly thick consistency, then brandy is added for flavour and as a preservative. Home-made there is nothing like it, and no mass-produced brand can compete.

Spread some spoonfuls of *Quedsche-Muus* on a slice of hearty, dark farmhouse bread, and just wait for what the local wasp population has to say about it. They will buzz with excitement!

Mrs. Gerber's teenage grandson, rarely seen otherwise, pays his granny a visit on the occasion of her seventieth birthday. Mrs. Gerber, extremely pleased about his appearance, turns to him lovingly saying: 'Now then, you deserve the place of honour at my birthday table. Where do you want to sit?'

One look at the table and promptly the answer comes: 'I'd better sit next to the *Quedsche-Kuche* . . . '

Raddegiggel

pronounced 'rudde(r)-giggle' to rhyme with 'mud a wriggle'. High German: Rattentöter. English: Plonk, sour wine.

One kind, and possibly the worst kind of wine is called *Raddegiggel*. It does all a good wine wouldn't, and doesn't do what a good wine should; instead of making you feel light-hearted and free of worries, it provides you with a bad taste in your mouth and a hangover of capital size the next day.

The very name makes you shudder as much as the wine itself. *Raddegiggel* means wriggling like a poisoned rat. No doubt a strong way of describing the effect of such wine, but you will know exactly why, should you happen to take a sip by chance. A wee bit kinder to your constitution comes what is called *Rachebutzer* (pronounced 'Ru*ch*-a-bou(l)dzer' – *ch* as in Scots 'lo*ch*' throat cleanser).

The nick-naming of wines is common in the Pfalz, where annually many millions of bottles are filled with the precious sap. Describing it in the first stage, prior to fermentation, when the cider is still turbid, the expression *Fedderweisser* (pronounced 'fedder-whysser' – feather white) is used. Or it is called *Bidsler* (sparkler – see also under B – *Bidselwasser*).

There is a world of difference between a bad, sour wine, one which we call 'a vintage of the côtes-du-vinaigre' (from the vinegar region) and a dry wine. The latter is sometimes labelled *Diabetiker-Wein* (spelled *Diabetigger* in the Pfalz, and pronounced 'dee-ah-beh-tigger', in English meaning 'suitable for diabetics'). Though low in sugar content, the *Diabetigger* is not recommendable to diabetics for medical reasons, and permission to use the term was withdrawn, but it is still in circulation.

Such dry wines have the advantage that they do not interfere with your stomach; something the *Radde-giggel* will do, giving you heart-burn, particularly if they come at too high a price.

Dry wines improve with age. But every palate develops its own preference and there will always be plenty of demand for the sweeter varieties of wine: For *Spätlese* (pronounced 'shpadt-lase(r)'), wine from grapes ripened longer on the vine. For *Auslese* (pronounced 'ous-lase(r)'), from specially selected grapes. For *Trockenbeerauslese* (pronounced 'trock-an-bear-ous-lase(r)'), from specially selected over-ripe grapes, inspected for fungi infestation and others beforehand. Or for *Eiswein* (pronounced 'ice-vine'), made from grapes picked after the first frost set in and crushed at near zero centigrade. Because of its scarcity and the involved process of its production, *Eiswein* is an obvious luxury and way on top of any price list.

Besides using proper names and coining nicknames for Pfälzer wines, the local vintners go one step further. Each year the ruling *Wine Queen* will baptize the new vintage. Here are some of the results arrived at after elaborate ceremonies of wine tasting and taking into account the general conditions and mood within the nation:

1931, a year of economic crisis: 'Crisling'.

1934, the year of the passing of the anti-semitic Nuremberg Laws: 'Noble Pedigree'.

1936, the year of re-armament for war: 'Recruit'.

1949, the year the Federal Republic was founded: 'Federal Brother'.

1958, the year of the Soviet Sputnik: 'Moon Jumper'.

Every year, into eternity, another wine thus baptized will be added to the collection.

Should any adulterator be caught while producing *Raddegiggel*, he can expect a heavy fine or more. If he is a real Pfälzer he will surely have the last word by quipping with a bit of self-irony: 'My wine they let run away, but I was jugged for six weeks.'

Saumaache

pronounced 'zow-maach-a' (ch *as in* 'loch') *to rhyme with 'brow-tar-a'. High German: Saumagen. English: Pig's stomach or maw.*

Over a hundred years ago, a poet by the name of Karl August Woll wrote thirty-six verses in praise of *Saumaache*, a favourite item on a Pfälzer menu card.

Don't comment on it, unless you've tried it. True, anything the Pfälzer vernacular connects with 'sau' (the generic term 'Schwein' is rarely used) usually takes on a negative or derogatory implication. Many curses and comparatives start with 'sau' to underline uncleanliness for instance ('saudreggich' – very dirty) or stupidity ('saubleed' – very stupid). But there are two exceptions: 'Saugligg' (pronounced 'zow-glig' – extreme good luck) and *Saumaache*.

For the recipe you would be well advised to consult a Pfälzer cookbook. For all we know, a lot of work goes into the preparation of what amounts to a super haggis – less the lamb and the Scots.

A restaurant in Germersheim is well known for the special way the dish is prepared there. On Monday the chef buys about thirty even-sized pig's maws directly from the slaughter house (even-sized so that they may be boiled at the same temperature for the same length of time without differing results). Cleaning the maws is the worst job. Tuesday, onions, potatoes, garlic cloves and more are peeled and chopped. Wednesday, meat of all sorts is cut into small cubes, eggs are broken, bags of herbs and spices emptied and the mixtures stirred together. Then the lot goes into the maws. Thursday morning the boiling starts. At dinner time, when the *Saumaache* have finally been baked in the oven to golden crispness, long rows of Mercedes cars from near and far line up, and everyone hopes to find a seat at crowded tables.

Saumaache enjoys such a high esteem that one of the best vineyards in the famous wine growing community of Kallstadt bottles its delicious Riesling under the designation of 'Kallstadter *Saumagen*' (for the consumers' sake in High German, of course).

The pigs in the Pfalz, which donate so generously their maws and other parts to the afore-mentioned delicacies, have a reputation of sturdiness. A farmhand, who had briefly interrupted his outdoor decorating and painting, returned to find his paint bucket empty. He suspected that some schoolboys had played a trick on him. But he was wrong. A white trail led from the empty bucket straight to the nearby enclosure, where the pigs were kept. The boar still exhibited a white snout, yet no trace of discomfort. Roaming about, the animal had come across the bucket and had helped himself freely.

Another boar, this time a wild one, helped himself freely, too. Though in quite a different way. His offence came to light, when a farmer discovered his gilt pregnant, in spite of the fact that he had kept her inside an eight-foot fence. The piglets showed every sign of being bastards, a cross between their domesticated mother and some wild representative of the species. The only conclusion permitted under the circumstances was that one amorous night a boar must have jumped the eight-foot fence. The villagers had a good laugh, while the farmer, thus 'cuckolded', was musing how the beast – once inside, driven by lust and ardour – had managed to get out of the enclosure in spite of weak knees.

Schaadefreed

pronounced 'Shahed-a-frehed' to rhyme with 'marmalade'. High German: Schadenfreude. English: A kind of malicious pleasure.

It has been said that the entire drama of existence – much like being drawn between the opposing forces of Good and Evil – is played out between the polarities of *Gemiedlichkeit* and *Schaadefreed* (for which there doesn't exist an English term in either case).

Where *Schaadefreed* starts, *Gemiedlichkeit* (High German: Gemütlichkeit, pronounced in Palatinate 'ga-mead-*lich*-kite' with *ch* as in Scots '*nicht*' – a cosy home atmosphere) comes to an end, as well as vice versa.

Schaadefreed is defined in most dictionaries as 'delight caused by the misfortune of others'.

The Pfälzer, however, have their own ways and manage, as so often, to reconcile extremes, even of that caliber. They learned how to change signs and accomplish a reversal from the negative into an entirely positive *Gemiedlichkeit*, as the following story will prove.

In a village school in the Wasgau, the instructor in religion also happened to be the local priest. One day, he gave his pupils enough written work to do that he found time for a smoke in the corridor. Suddenly he couldn't resist spying on his flock to see, whether they were really diligent. In order to do that he climbed out of the corridor window and up on to the roof.

No sooner was he up there than the children spotted him and were on their best behaviour. Satisfied with the discipline in his class the priest decided to climb back. Yet, with his over-weight problem and because of his theological rather than physical training, he found just that impossible.

The bell rang and all the children swarmed out to stare at their teacher up on the roof. No noise, no wise-cracks – and no-one ran to fetch help. Only when the caretaker spotted the clergyman in his misfortune, was he helped down.

Naturally this occurrence made hilarious news and soon everybody in the village chuckled with suppressed laughter about the trapped nosy Parker. This was – to an extent – *Schaadefreed*, and well deserved at that.

However the mayor, a just man, remained unconvinced and made up his mind to put the silly story to a test. For him it was nothing but anti-religious slander aimed against the Church.

In possession of a key to the school-house, he entered the building after night-fall. He searched for the window in question and with the help of a chair found it indeed easy enough to get out and on to the roof. No time remained for further ponderings. A draught in the corridor had banged the window shut. The bolt snapped.

Over an hour passed before the good man spotted someone in the darkness and yelled for help. The passer-by, a villager, ran to sound the fire-alarm as soon as he learned who was up there. Out came the fire-brigade in full, followed by all and sundry. Amidst much shouting and laughing the mayor was lowered from his uncomfortable position on the school-house roof.

Anywhere else, this story would have resulted in endless *Schaadefreed*. But be it borne in mind that all this happened in the Pfalz. What did the mayor do? Once back on safe ground again, he invited the fire-brigade and anyone else who cared to come along into the Wirtschaft (see under letter W – *Woi*) for a drink at his expense. And it turned out an evening of *Gemiedlichkeit*, after all.

Schneggenuudel

pronounced 'shneg-a-noodle' to rhyme with 'leg o' poodle'. High German: Schnecke (Kaffeegebäck). English: A type of Danish pastry.

A Pfälzer love song begins: 'Du bischt moi *Schneggenuudel*, du bischt moi Zuggerschnuut' (meaning: You are my *Schneggenuudel*, you are my sugar snout). Need anything more be said about the Pfälzer's sweet tooth and the way it enhances their poetic imagination?

The *Schneggenuudel* is baked in the shape of a large spiral or 'Schnegg' (i.e. snail). Apart from the fact that it is made from dough, it has nothing whatsoever in common with vermicelli, macaroni or spaghetti or any other noodle type of *Nuudel*. You may have it glazed, with icing, or if you prefer filled with chopped almonds, cinnamon and raisins.

Being part of a whole family of culinary delicacies in South-West Germany, the *Schneggenuudel* counts among its relations the *Fasnachts-Kiechel*, a deep-fried doughnut prepared during the carnival season (see also under letter N – *Närrischkeit*), and the *Dambnuudel*, a sort of steamed dumpling. The *Dambnuudel* appears on the Pfälzer dinner table rather regularly: on Fridays when traditions calls for a meatless dish (much like the *Quedsche-Kuche* with potato soup, its competitor during the *Quedsche* season – see also under Q – *Quedsch*). Delicious with wine sauce or – in its salty version – with anything for supper, the *Dambnuudel* is a hit on any occasion. And you will find the recipe in any South-West German cookbook. Each housewife uses her own inherited variation of the recipe.

In the old village of Oppau, now integrated into the township of Ludwigshafen, the *Dambnuudel* has a prominent place within the local folklore.

Once upon a time a lady from Oppau prepared her *Dambnuudle* (plural and pronounced 'dump-noode-le'), set them into the customary black iron pot, put the lid on and left the dumplings steaming on the kitchen range. Having some errands to do, she left the house, and was soon caught up in urgent gossip with a friend.

In the meanwhile, the local fire-brigade was answering a call to a house, from which dark smoke was rising. They forced their way into the dwelling and found the culprit: the very iron pot with *Dambnuudle* burnt beyond recognition, the black center piece in a cloud of smoke. Ever since, the people of Oppau have been nicknamed the *Dambnuudle*, and, carrying the name with grace, they even passed it on to their carnival club.

Let us briefly return to the *Schneggenuudel*, though. Its peculiar shape gave a Mannheim baker an idea, which led to another typically Pfälzische speciality. During the last century the municipal council of Mannheim declared that further street cleaning services would be dependent on a sizeable rate increase. Out came the Pfälzer in protest, and said baker with a new kind of pastry. Dark in colour and similar to the *Schneggenuudel* in size and shape, made from nuts and fruit and chocolate, *Mannemer Dreck* appeared in his shop window, small, brown and scrumptious heaps of dirt from Mannheim. What a way to get even with the council and to satirize inappropriate cuts in service.

The problem was solved peacefully, and a few

selected and 'copy-righted' bakeries still sell this sweet joke to tourists and to the locals alike.

The intertwined and complicated pattern of access roads to the Rhine bridge between Mannheim and Ludwigshafen evoked such a familiar image in the Pfälzer's mind that they couldn't help nicknaming the bridge *Schneggenuudel-Brigg*. (Though first claim to fame belongs to the foot-bridge across a Ludwigshafen harbour basin.)

Schlabbe

pronounced 'schlub-a' to rhyme with 'rub a'. High German: Hausschuhe. English: Slippers.

Whether in the singular or plural, *Schlabbe* never changes its grammatical form, even though in contrast the shape of *Schlabbe* does with wear.

Schlabbe owe their existence to a time of need. In days gone by farmers wore wooden clogs carved locally by talented wood workers. Such solid foot-wear was guaranteed water-proof, mud-resistant and easy to slip into or out of. The mountain region of the Wasgau up to Pirmasens supplied the wood that went into these clogs (with plenty enough over for the wooden vine-props used in the Pfalz and exported in great numbers to other wine-growing areas).

Leather shoes were expensive, out of range of the poor farmers so often struck by bad harvests. So the women-folk started to make soft house-shoes from left-over bits and pieces of material that were called *Schlabbe*, which means 'flabby' and 'soft'. Little wonder that 'to have your *Schlabbe* on' is synonymous with being in the cosy comfort of your (or anyone else's) home.

In accordance with their love for exaggeration and teasing (see also under I – *Iwwerdreiwe* and U – *Uudse*) the Pfälzer will use the word *Schlabbe* in numerous ways and combinations. A threat larger than life and never followed up by action is: 'I beat you up, until no

Schlabbe will fit you!' To be on the safe side, the one so addressed may do well 'to run until his *Schlabbe* are flying.' Should he be too much of a coward to even run for cover, he is a *Schlabbschwanz* (or 'a flabby tail', which has the obvious double meaning, too).

Pirmasens, today the centre of West Germany's shoe manufacturing industry, quite naturally – it is after all situated in the Pfalz – bears the name *Schlabbefligger-fawwrik* (slipper repair factory), while its inhabitants are called the *Schlabbefligger*, what else? The *Schlabbe-fliggerfawwrik* has done well for itself. Annually a large Leather Fair is held in its boundaries and a lot of work done in its factories is commissioned from Italy and from as far out as India.

It was Pirmasens where a music teacher from Ludwigs-hafen had accepted the offer to conduct the youth orchestra. A man of genius, he never minded the clock. All of a sudden he realized that he had to catch the train to Pirmasens in just under ten minutes. He changed with the speed of lightening into his tails and ran to the nearby station (then still in the centre of town). Settling down in his compartment he straightened his tie, brushed a few specks of dust from his suit, pulled up his socks – and realized he was still wearing his *Schlabbe*!

Unimaginable what our musicus would have done or how he would have dealt with the situation, had his destination been any other than Pirmasens. There, of course, he found – among the many *Schlabbefligger* – one who carried his size of patent leather shoes and didn't mind to be called to serve him, way after closing hour.

Schdroossebah(n)

pronounced 'shdro(r)ce-a-ba(r)(n)' to rhyme with 'fo(r)ce a khan'. High German: Strassenbahn. English: Tram-car.

No more versatile academy to further studies in the Palatinate dialect than a *Schdroossebah(n)*. Calculate a bit of waiting time in. But anyhow, that is time well spent, too. At the stop you will get recompensated already, for Pfälzer are never shy and start a conversation anywhere. Once aboard, there is no avoiding getting to know them. It may prove worthwhile to start the conversation yourself, with *Horschemol* or *Horsche Se mol* (see under letter H) and a question, and then wait for things to happen. With a smile and such an opening the ice is broken immediately.

Ludwigshafen and Mannheim run their *Schdroossebah(n)* system jointly. It is fast and efficient and a matter of great pride for all, particularly for those who cannot afford a motor car or won't use it in town because of parking problems.

Nowadays tickets are sold by vending machines. Yet in times past the driver stopped the car, the conductor jumped off, each passenger was given a ticket cranked out of a little contraption for the exact amount of points needed for the distance, and the entire venture was one of Gemiedlichkeit (see under S – *Schaadefreed*).

After the 'Firy Elias', a miniature local railway that linked the various parts of the spreading town of

Ludwigshafen, the electrical tram-cars (also called 'Elekdrisch' or 'sparky carriage') were a great improvement. The former had let off enormous clouds of smoke from its coal-fired engine. When it jumped off the track, it had to be put back on its trail by hand levers. But even so, the electrical *Schdroossebah(n)* like electrification of the towns altogether, was met with fearful distrust. Only after a period of adjustment did every newly built extension occasion a local celebration with flags and public speeches and the lot.

A posher version of the *Schdroossebah(n)*, a kind of electrical commuter train, serves between Bad Dürkheim and Ludwigshafen (the 'Rhein-Haardt-Bahn') and between Mannheim and Heidelberg-Weinheim (the 'Oberrheinische Elektrizitäts-Gesellschaft' or 'O.E.G.' for short).

For him, who chases after women as a matter of instinct, the phrase was coined: 'If the *Schdroossebah(n)* would wear an apron, he would be running after it, too . . .'

Seppl is short for Joseph. And such a Seppl from a Pfälzer village came to town on a *Schdroossebah(n)*. When getting off while the car was still in motion, he went for the wrong handle and promptly fell – bottom down – into a soft heap of horse manure.

Enraged about his passenger's carelessness the conductor yelled at Seppl: 'It says here, in big, bold letters: "Hold on to the left handle-bar with your left hand, when descending." '

'Are you crazy?' Seppl replied: 'Do you want me to land face down in this mess, do you . . .?'

Tee

pronounced 'teh' to rhyme with 'he(y)'. High German: Tee. English: Tea.

By way of an apology for what English people have been getting, when they asked for a cup of tea in the Pfalz, let me give you some unusual and often overlooked facts: Ludwigshafen and Mannheim are relatively large ports, and Speyer and Worms have port facilities as well, a bit smaller in size, though.

That doesn't exactly make the Pfälzer into sea-farers. But it assures that they can directly import their type of *Tee*. It comes as 'Schwarzer *Tee*', the black tea of the Russian variety. Their tea ought to be served with lemon. It just doesn't taste right with milk.

Tee is shipped up the Rhine to Ludwigshafen and Mannheim (ports that take second place in size and cargo capacity only to the largest German inland port of Duisburg), and then it is stored in the huge warehouses along the river. With the import of *Tee*, strange images have reached the Pfalz from the North as well. 'Er hot ähner im *Tee*' is said of someone who is drunk, meaning 'he has something' – perhaps a jigger of rum – 'in his tea.'

Besides 'schwarzer *Tee*' the non-suspecting patron of a restaurant or café may be served a pot of herbal *Tee*, should the order not have explicitly stated otherwise. It might be *Pefferminztee* or *Kamilletee* or even *Hagebuddetee*, tea made from garden mint, camomile or rose-hip.

No wonder that the Pfälzer's opinion of these beverages is not the highest. They are sure that he, who drinks tea is on his way to his sick-bed, or worse to hospital. And once the habit of drinking tea has been started, there is no turning back. He is a write-off for good company, condemned for all eternity.

A retired bachelor from Wörth, who was being looked after by his housekeeper Therese, was warned by his doctor that his days would be counted if he didn't totally abstain from alcohol. 'What am I to drink, when I'm thirsty?' he protested. '*Tee*,' the doctor ordered, unmoved. 'Preferably *Pefferminztee* . . .'

In autumn, when the new wine was getting ready, the poor man just couldn't resist. He broke every promise he had made to his doctor, he broke it once, twice and once more again – until early in the morning, with an angelic smile of bliss and innocence he sank into the grassy ditch alongside the road that should have taken him home.

As it happened, a pensioned war officer walked his Great Dane, as usual, along that very road not an hour later. The animal was roaming around, discovered the blissful sleeper, gave him a sniff, turned and raised its hind leg.

Thus awakened and feeling a warm jet of liquid in his face, our friend blinked with one eye at the rising sun, groaned and murmured reproachfully: 'Please, Therese, this morning anything but *Pefferminztee* . . .'

Uudse

pronounced 'oods-a' to rhyme with 'shoots a'. High German: Uzen, necken. English: To tease.

It goes along well with the joyous, cheerful character of the Pfälzer that they do not miss an occasion to tease one another. Teasing and nicknaming go hand in hand, and there is plenty of evidence in the Pfalz of either or both.

A great Pfälzer painter and poet, a contemporary of Goethe, used the word as early as 1776 in his dramatic scenes of *The Life of Faustus*. But already 200 years before Maler Müller's (the painter-poet's name) time, *Uz* existed as the abbreviated form of the first name Ulrich. You never know, how things originate.

Though almost forgotten today, older generations of villagers still remember one of their favourite games as children, the *Uuds* of sending someone 'Elwedritsche fange' – to catch the mysterious E. The game is conducted along the same lines as the one that ends in the hunt for a Scottish hagtesse . . .

Uuds-names have a long tradition and were originally used to mislead the devil, should he come looking for someone in particular. Thus Joseph became Seppl, Fritz became Itzer (from the Hebrew name Itzhok), and Ulrich became *Uz*. It didn't stop there, of course, the inhabitants of whole towns would acquire their very descriptive *Uuds*-name, to which the *Schlabbefligger* of Pirmasens (see also under S – *Schlabbe*) can attest. Today it is the Carnival clubs that see to it that the old nicknames are not forgotten (see also under S – *Schneggenuudel* and the reference to the *Dambnuudle* of Oppau).

It is plausible that the natives of Altrip, a settlement founded by the Romans on the embankment of the Rhine, should be called the 'Moorhens' or in Pfälzisch 'de Wasserhinkle'. But why are the people of the village of Edigheim called 'the Slovacs'? Edigheim (the Pfälzer call it 'Edigum; pronounced 'eh-dig-'em) is also situated on the Rhine, and as the saying goes, 'Don't buy a cow from Edigum!' Nonsensical? No! Neither the saying nor the nickname are. There is something real beneath every *Uuds*. For one, Edigheim used to be situated in the middle of swampy pastures and the cattle population would come down with swamp fever inadvertently, so it was advisable not to buy a cow from there. And then, in the 18th century, under order of the elector palatine Carl Theodor (see under C) navvies from as far away as Bohemia came into these parts to dig a canal. They intermarried with the locals, and quite naturally Pfälzer customs mixed with some from Eastern Europe. The *Uuds*-name stuck, even though today that type of teasing still evokes mixed feelings in *Edigum*.

Children's rhymes like the one following are used for teasing in the streets:

O do dro
Kablemende mo.
Kablemende Idalian.
O do dro.

The kids accompany this seeming nonsense with fits of laughter, not knowing, what in fact they were saying. Little would they recognize the original, a French dance instructor's commands when teaching the steps of *La Française:*

Un, deux, trois,
Compliment à moi,
Compliment à l'Italien,
Un, deux, trois.

At times it doesn't matter that the *Uudser* reveals ignorance, as long as there is laughter in it for all.

Vertele

pronounced 'Ferrtle-a' to rhyme with 'revelle(r)'. High German: Viertelchen. English: A quarter of a liter (of wine).

There are four *Vertele* to each full liter of wine. Quartering the liter that way has many an advantage. For one, 0.25 liter quite logically comes to more than the skimpy little mouthful of wine served in 0.1 liter glasses most everywhere outside the *Pfalz*. An insult to the thirsty Palatinates! Moreover, the Pfälzer can order two *Vertele* at once, enough to fill the large cylindric *Schobbe*-glass. This saves time and the waiter an extra trip, at least until the next order of half a liter.

Vertele is the diminutive form of *Vertel* (and therefore is but a 'little' quarter). What warm affection, even adoration the Pfälzer expresses with the diminutive! His dog he will call a 'Hundele' (doggy), his house a 'Heisele' (little house), his girlfriend his 'Herzele' (little heart). But dearest to his heart is that little quarter of wine that can so easily be multiplied.

Nothing but the quarter measure will do. Heated arguments ensued among the locals, when silly new measurements were introduced, such as the 0.7 liter bottles of wine (not even three full quarters!), or glasses imitating the old Roman style but holding but 0.2 or even as little as 0.1 liter instead of a *Vertele* (or 0.25 liter) of wine. Whole teams of regular customers changed their trough out of protest. Others forced their innkeeper to retain the good measure for the members of the *Stammtisch* (the round-table regulars) at least.

Most Pfälzer frequent their very own *Stammtisch*, gathering at a given hour to chat with their cronies and have a *Vertele* or two or three. 'He is going to his eleven o'clock service' does therefore not refer to a pious church-goer but to a regular on his way to the *Stammtisch*.

Vertele are not gulped down but sipped with all due ceremony they will teach you during wine tastings. In old taverns you may still find wooden tables with an inlaid centre of sedimentary rock on which the glasses, jugs or bottles are set. The stone serves as a marvelous 'cooler'.

The number of *Vertele* a man can consume depends on his training, his stamina and of course on the quality of the wine. A man with a nose like a red bulb is never scolded for excessive drinking, he rather enjoys the reputation of having his *Vertele* blossoming in his face.

The number of *Vertele*, too, determines a Pfälzer's reaction and action. This is best illustrated by the story of the sober cat and the tipsy mouse.

A wine-jolly mouse fell into a wine cask and paddled for dear life. 'Help! Help!' it yelled to the sober cat. 'Save me! Better to be eaten by you than to drown here.'

The cat rescued the mouse out of its predicament. Then, one jump and the mouse disappeared in its hole.

'You rotten liar!' the cat hissed angrily. 'What about your promise that I could eat you?'

Whispered the wine-jolly mouse from its hole: 'You see, it's all this drinking. When I made my promise to you, I had one *Vertele* too many . . . '

How true the Palatinate proverb: 'First I gave him my promise, and now he even wants me to keep it . . . '

By the way, the Pfälzer love their *Vertele* filled well

above the mark engraved near the top of the quarter liter glass.

Woi

pronounced 'voy' to rhyme with 'joy'. High German: Wein. English: Wine.

There is one method of verifying the ethnic background of the Pfälzer which is scientifically superior to any other – the one that bases its result on the sampling of their blood. Should the sample reveal more proof of *Woi* than of blood, all doubt is removed, the person is a true Palatinate. This method is known under the name of *Woi-Prob* (wine sampling).

It is obviously futile to try to say anything conclusive about *Woi* in a few lines. Just consider the thirty or so types of wine quality alone that are listed in every learned book on the subject. However, one fact remains true, and in a round-about way every promotional pamphlet from any *Woi* region in Germany attests to it by stating: We are the largest wine growing area *with the exception of the Pfalz*!

The most comprehensive permanent exhibition of anything to do with *Woi*, throughout the millenia, can be viewed in the famous Weinmuseum of Speyer. There are geographical maps with names of vineyards nobody in his sober mind would ever dream of deciphering. Hidden behind the names on bottle labels describing *Woi* of various localities, types and vintages there is a whole wealth of information about the etymological, botanical, zoological and even religious history.

With his bottle of Riesling the connoisseur will

savour the knowledge that the Riesling grape was first mentioned on a parchment bearing the date 1490. What dimension is added to the enjoyment of a beverage that contains more than just alcohol. For those who treasure the art of wine growing and drinking the rococo of castles in ruin, the romanticism of quiet valleys, the memory of gothic horrors, baroque pleasures, ancient sagas and legends and the long lost Golden Age come along with the *Woi*.

Of course, wine making has become such a big industry that the Pfalz can base a sizeable part of its budget on the revenue from wine sales. In turn the vintners are shrewdly aware of the economics of their trade. While generous and hospitable with their precious sap in private, they must also be callously calculating when it comes to selling their vintage to the public, all the time saving enough for their own consumption.

In Edenkoben it was that a Pfälzer wine lover lost a 50p piece from his purse. Others kindly pointed this out to him. 'For a 50p coin you want me to bend down?' he asked. 'If I do that,' the Pfälzer continued, 'wine for ten times that amount will pour out of me!'

Woi has over the centuries been a most favoured subject of the poets, who bear but little likeness otherwise to the ancient god Bacchus. None could sing more movingly about *Woi* and *Wertschaft* (pronounced 'verrt-shuft'. High German: Wirtshaus. English: Wine tavern) than Kurt Dehn from the Pfalz. He was able to express the Pfälzer's deepest fear and dearest hope by sighing:

> Wenn in dem grosse Himmel bloss
> ä klääni Wertschaft wär.

> If only there were in that big heaven above
> a little wine tavern.

The song one of us contributed on the subject has three strangers discover certain mathematical peculiarities when they leave a Pfälzer *Wertschaft*. They see everything double, which makes six of them, each one with four legs – which adds up to 24 legs between them. On their 24 legs the three in a set of six sway happily home: while the *Woi* has shown its power by creating new laws of multiplication.

Mind you – the one who wrote these lyrics was thrown out of school at an early age because of his performance in Math.

Worscht

pronounced 'vorsht' to rhyme with 'scorched'.
High German: Wurst. English: Sausage.

'*Worscht* makes thirsty, and thirst makes hungry' is a rather typical saying in the Pfalz. It describes the vicious circle in which the Pfälzer seem to rotate to no end.

Worscht exists in so many varieties that a sense of proportion and humility forbids their introduction in detail. One type looks like English bangers, tastes quite differently and comes in pairs: the pale-skinned *Broodworscht* (pronounced 'broad vorsht', 'Bratwurst' in High German and 'frying sausage' in English). Then there is the princess of sausages, strictly for heating up in simmering water: The pínk-skinned *Servelat* (which in the Pfalz begs to differ from any other of said name anywhere else). As a gift from France, or rather from the Huguenots who introduced French-style paté, the famous *Lewwerworscht* (pronounced 'levver vorsht', 'Leberwurst' in High German, 'liver sausage' in English) deserves mention – not only because many a happy gourmet has been relishing the taste involuntarily throughout the night.

Moreover, there is a black pudding-style *Bluudworscht* or *Blunz* (pronounced 'blued vorscht' or 'bloonts') which changes its name into *Grieweworscht* (pronounced 'grieve-a-vorsht) as well as its texture, taste and colour scheme, once bits of fat are added to the mixture. Another delicacy is *Lewwerkees* (pronounced 'levver-caisse', meaning 'liver cheese', but lacking any relationship at all to cheese as we know it).

Bad Dürkheim is number one, when it comes to celebrating the *Worscht* (see also under D – *Derkhem* and its *Worschtmarkt*).

Asked to name three high holidays in the Pfalz, a native is reported to have answered: 'Holy Fun Fair Day', 'Holy Wine Tasting' and 'Holy Slaughter Day' (in reverence to all the *Worscht* made on the occasion).

During the time, when pigs were still slaughtered in the farm yard (rare today), a broth was made with all of the *Worscht* fillings that had burst out of the skin. The soup was ladled into pots and pans and sent – as *Worschtsupp* – to the village poor and to the appreciative neighbours.

To give notice of the big event that slaughterday still represents, a pig's bladder, inflated like a balloon, may be fastened above the house door. Should you see the sign and feel inclined, do knock on the door and ask for half a pound of *Hausmacher Worscht* (home-made sausage). Without much ado the family will usually sell you the portion desired.

Besides the fact that *Weck* (rolls made of white flour), *Worscht* and *Woi* (see under letter W – *Woi*) lend themselves readily as a line of poetic alliteration, folks couldn't resist immortalizing *Worscht*, even if it meant parodying a famous Eichendorff poem and folksong:

> Wem Gott will rechte Gunscht erweise,
> den schickt er in die *Worscht*fawwrik.
> Er losst'n in die *Worscht* noi beisse
> un gebt'm noch e Schtickel mit

> If God will grace you with His favour,
> He'll send you where the *Worscht* is made.

He'll let you have a bite of any flavour
and gives you some for on the way.

And at the point, where you couldn't care less about what's up or down, because you've had enough, you can say in the best of Pfälzisch: 'Mir is alles Worscht!' (pronounced 'mere is ull-a-ss vorsht', meaning 'All is sausage to me').

Xuntheid

pronounced 'ksou(l)nt-hide' to rhyme with 'bush glide'. High German: Gesundheit. English: Good health. Bless you!

While the English will say 'Bless you!' to one who sneezes, the Pfälzer will exclaim 'Xuntheid'. Both, the blessing and the good health wished for, go back to the very early incantations that were to break the evil spell and drive away the demon that made you sneeze. They are, in a way, examples of atavistic customs still with us today.

Bless the peculiar Palatinate pronunciation ever so slightly off the High German normal one of 'Gesundheit' ('ge-zou(l)nd-hite') for without it the letter X would have been a lot harder to deal with. But given the contraction of High German 'Ges . . . ' to the Palatinate 'X . . . ' there are quite a few other words that start with this letter, such as: Xangvarroin (High German: Gesangverein, English: Glee club), Xindel (High German: Gesindel, English: Riff-raff), Xox (High German: G'socks, from the Yiddish for riff-raff) and xalse (High German: Gesalzen, English: Salted) as in 'xalseni Rechnung' (High German: Gesalzene Rechnung, English: A stiff bill or unexpected high invoice).

Here is a short list of what the Pfälzer consider good for their *Xuntheid*:

xund is – everything the doctor prescribes, the chemist

sells, plus all you do to disprove either or both.

- to wash your hands before every meal to get rid of the bacteria, also not to wash your hands in order to toughen up against bacteria.
- to wear thermal underwear during any season, because what helps against the cold is also useful against the heat.
- to complain that there is a draught, wherever you sit or stand, as precaution is better than pneumonia.
- to have a cat handy against rheumatism.
- rising early, or, if that doesn't help, sleeping late.
- a stiff westerly breeze, as it brings ozone from the forests of the Pfälzer Wald.
- to sweep the road clear of snow, thus preventing slipping.
- to avoid drinking beer after wine, to steer clear of adulterated wine and too much foreign food.
- a cup of herbal tea against everything, stewed rhubarb against the very same.
- to disbelieve everything you read in the papers, hear on the radio or see on television, though seeing at times may be believing.
- to force young left-handers to use their right hands as well as to obey traffic signals regardless whether there is traffic or not – both save a lot of trouble in life.
- to have a good laugh about yourself from time to time, and most of the time have one about others.
- cutting inner soles out of newspapers to put into your shoes, eating regular meals and turning off the gas during thunderstorms.

- to wear a hat one size too big and a shirt with a collar one size too small, all for better blood circulation.
- to outdo everyone in taking care of your health BUT BE CAREFUL, DON'T KILL YOURSELF DOING IT! XUNTHEID!

Yoyo

pronounced 'yoh-yoh'. High German: Jaja. English: Isn't it? Is this so? O well! (With a slight intonation of disbelief)

Yoyo may at first sight and sound remind us of the Japanese art of making a disk jump up and down a thin string. And after all, is the Pfalz not such a treasure chest of historical, cultural and etymological peculiarities that you may easily expect something Japanese? Besides, every spring cherry and almond trees blossom in the Pfalz in such abundance that a Japanese poet would be filled with delight.

Yoyo, however, like its more affirmative counterpart *heiyo* (pronounced 'hi-yoh', meaning something like 'well yes') bears witness to the (rare) occurrence of the letter Y in the Palatinate alphabet. Furthermore, it is these little words, these in-between fillers, that puzzle the foreign visitor. What is their function, their precise meaning? Can they be used without exposing oneself to ridicule? Logical analysis helps little, the best way is to listen to the natives:

'Pleased to see you, and your daughter!' the old-age pensioner diplomatically greeted the mayor strolling through a public park in the company of a very young woman.

'O no!' the mayor responded proudly. 'Please meet my wife.'

'*Yoyo*?' muttered the old fellow, barely hiding his disbelief.

This sceptical employment of the expression is emphasized by a slight raising of one's voice. In this way, the Pfälzer can call most everything into question, subtly but unmistakably.

'What's the matter with old Max?' a villager enquired turning to his school-time friend now also in his seventies.

'Didn't you know? They first took him to Neustadt into hospital, and then he died there last week.'

'Yoyo?!' the former replied shaking his head. 'Is this why one doesn't see much of him these days?'

Recently we came across an interesting item regarding the letter Y. It makes one of its rare appearances in the name of the town of *Speyer*, and this only since early last century. In earlier documents the same town goes under the name of Speier.

Apparently the substitution of y for i took place not long after the Congress of Vienna in 1814/1815, when the Pfalz was made part of the kingdom of Bavaria. Until then the name for Bavaria, too, was written with the letter i and read 'Baiern'. Yet as the King of Bavaria, Maximilian Joseph, saw one of his sons ascending to the throne of Greece, he felt he owed something to Greek culture, took the letter y from the Greek alphabet and exchanged it for the letter i and called himself 'König von Bayern.'

And *Speyer*?

The citizens' council followed suit and changed the town's name from *Speier* to *Speyer* out of reverence for their Bavarian ruler. (At about the same time, and for the very same reason, Jewish families throughout the Bavarian kingdom changed their name from 'Meier' or 'Maier' to 'Meyer' or 'Mayer'.)

The change didn't matter much.

'Is *Speyer* what it always was?' a former Palatinate asked a resident of the town. 'I mean – alive and well only because of the imperial tombs in the Cathedrale?'

'Heiyo!' was the answer, in the affirmative.

Zwock'l

pronounced 'tsvockle' to rhyme with 'cockle'.
Palatinate for a Bavarian.

Should the part of the world you come from be officially referred to as the 'garden of Germany', soon somebody will set his mind to getting into it.

The offical who referred to it in these terms was a Bavarian king, and by the time he coined the phrase, he had already gotten into it, in fact, he had gotten it.

Suddenly and by the ruling of a European conference (the Congress of Vienna of 1814/1815) the Pfalz saw itself in the possession of the Wittelsbacher, the royal dynasty in charge of Bavaria. No relationship to them had existed before.

From 1816 onward, King Maximilian Joseph commissioned a certain Franz Xaver von Zwackh to run the Pfalz in the interest of Munich, capital of the Bavarian monarchy. (Until the year 1945, every Pfälzer remained a citizen of the state of Bavaria.) In disrespectful reference to Herr von Zwackh the Palatinates from that time on called the Bavarians *Zwock'l*! So one story goes.

The other explanation for *Zwock'l* may acquit Herrn von Zwackh as the model for the nick-name. In Frankonia, too, the Bavarians are known as *Zwock'l*, though Herr von Zwackh never had any jurisdiction over that part of the country. But the Franks at one time suffered the same fate as the Pfälzer, they, too, were annexed to the Bavarian Crown. And the 'Royal Bavarian Officers' on duty in the Pfalz, in Frankonia and elsewhere wore fancy uniforms, with two silver twiglets flashing on their cockade. These twiglets ('Zwoagerln' in Bavarian, 'Zweiglein' in High German) may actually be the culprits responsible for *Zwock'l*, which goes to show that the Bavarians are themselves responsible for their Pfälzer (and Frankish) nick-name.

Now, with this little book coming to an end, let us look once more at the Pfälzer. They are bright people, no book is needed to prove that. Often enough during their history they have proven it themselves. In spite of – or may-be because of – the ever-changing forces of occupation, they are a freedom-loving people, and a clever one in avoiding all too keen cooperation with the various tax collectors they had to answer to.

So it was during the ruling days of the *Zwock'l*. Every barrel of wine was heavily taxed. Only stolen wine was exempted, and logically, everything smuggled out of the country could neither be traced nor taxed.

Accordingly an innkeeper of Limburgerhof reported a cart-load of wine stolen from him to the *Zwock'l* tax collector. So vividly was he able to describe the thieves that the Bavarian official was convinced, while the Pfälzer laughed in his sleeves and counted his money.

But as with all misdeeds that remain undetected, this one too came under the rule of the evil spirits. As punishment thieves began haunting the roads and graveyards around Limburgerhof. They can still be seen there, at midnight when the moon is full. Yet only those with an absolutely clean conscience with regard to their tax statements will be able to observe the apparition.

Perhaps it is for that reason: Sighting of these ghosts of Pfälzer wine thieves is reported rarely nowadays . . .

Index of Names

Index of Places and Peoples

Table of Contents *Page*

Table of Contents *Page*

ARNO REINFRANK

Ein Butler aus der Pfalz

1992, gebunden, 160 Seiten

Der seit 1955 in London ansässige Autor schildert die bewegte Lebensgeschichte eines nach England ausgewanderten Pfälzers. Nicht nur das typische englische Schlangestehen, der Linksverkehr, das Teetrinken, die Weihnachtsbräuche werden treffsicher aus pfälzer Sicht auf's Korn genommen.
Auch die Erfahrungen mit der englischen Weiblichkeit, das Rasenmähen, Überraschungen bei einer Versteigerung und bei der Fuchsjagd wird der Leser mit dem "Helden" dieses Buches miterleben.
Daß dabei kein Auge trocken bleibt, dafür steht der Name Arno Reinfrank.

ARNO REINFRANK

übrigens: Die Pfalz

1993, Kt., 96 Seiten

Auf verblüffend neuartige Weise zeigt der seit 1955 in London ansässige Autor seine Heimatverbundenheit. In "vier Dialogen", ähnlich dem alten Sokrates, umkreist er seine Themen, um zu einer modernen Klärung dessen beizutragen, was "die Pfalz" uns allen bedeutet. Schlitzohrig teilt er diese Aufgabe einem "hochdeutschen" Akademiker und einem "urpälzer" Arbeiter zu, deren Äußerungen um so komischer wirken, weil jeder sich selbst karikiert. Angesprochen sind nicht nur Ortsbestimmung und Mentalität der Pfalz und ihrer Bewohner. Es geht auch um die Entsorgung der Landschaft von Industriemüll und Skin-Heads, und um das Bestreben "Weck, Worscht un Wei" nicht allein die kulturelle Szene besetzen zu lassen.